housebeautiful
decorating *style*

housebeautiful
decorating *style*

the Editors of

HOUSE BEAUTIFUL
MAGAZINE

text by

CAROL COOPER GAREY

Hearst Books ❖ A Division of Sterling Publishing Co., Inc. ❖ New York

Copyright © 1992 by Hearst Communications, Inc.

Produced by Smallwood & Stewart Inc., New York City
Edited by Susan E. Davis
Designed by Michelle Wiener

Library of Congress Cataloging-in-Publication Data
Available upon request.

10   9   8   7   6   5   4   3   2   1

Published by Hearst Books,
A Division of Sterling Publishing Co., Inc.
387 Park Avenue South, New York, N.Y. 10016

House Beautiful and Hearst Books are trademarks owned by
Hearst Magazines Property, Inc., in USA,
and Hearst Communications, Inc., in Canada.

Distributed in Canada by Sterling Publishing
C/o Canadian Manda Group, One Atlantic Avenue, Suite 105
Toronto, Ontario, Canada M6K 3E7
Distributed in Australia by Capricorn Link (Australia) Pty. Ltd.
P.O. Box 704, Windsor, NSW 2756 Australia

Printed in China

ISBN 1-58816-199-4

CONTENTS

THE ESSENTIALS

THE ELEMENTS

THE DETAILS

GREAT TRANSFORMATIONS

introduction

Decorating and style, the two words that make up the title of this book, are intricately intertwined, yet, at the same time, very different. Decorating is a discipline, an applied art, a set of skills that involves a knowledgeable manipulation of space, an arrangement of objects within that space, and the solving of specific design problems. The problem can be one or many: too little light, a lack of handsome proportions, a purpose for the space that limits the arrangement of furniture. Style, on the other hand, is more personal, more a question of taste and preference. It is a point of view, an attitude, a unique background—all the things that give a room personality, hopefully, your personality. For style is really what makes a room yours. And it is only when these two parts—decorating and style—come together in a room that decorating style is achieved.

Decorating style is what *House Beautiful* has been reporting on for almost 100 years. This book reflects hundreds of examples of stylish decorating discovered by our decorating editors and chosen because they seem to suit our lives today. We've organized the book into four parts: first a chapter on the Essentials that illustrate basic decorating building blocks: harmony, color, scale. From there we move to the Elements: the parts of a room that must come together if a room is going to work. And we've covered all of them, with ideas for walls and windows, floors and ceilings, and the architectural detailing that may be missing, or there but unwelcome, which can be either enhanced or disguised.

The third chapter focuses more closely on the style half of the equation. Dozens of examples of Details were chosen specifically to fuel your imagination and help you recognize how a personal collection, some treasured family pieces, art you value, or your way with flowers can help give your room personal style. In the fourth and final chapter, we look at five American houses where we found personal style and accomplished decorating meshed in a way that illustrates what we mean by decorating style. You'll find the five Great Transformations are very different, but equally successful—and the one you like best will tell you a lot about your own true decorating style.

Throughout the book we have chosen beautiful photographs that focus on all the ingredients that give these spaces style. Carol Cooper Garey's text explains what makes each scheme work and elaborates on the ideas the pictures contain. Our goal throughout was the same we have in editing *House Beautiful* each month: to help you make your rooms more beautiful, to enhance your quest for decorating style.

THE EDITORS
House Beautiful

CHAPTER ONE

THE ESSENTIALS

harmony, color, and scale

The success of a room is due to the sum of its parts: the proportions, the number and shape of the windows, the quality of light, the architectural details. Transforming a naked room into a comfortable, visually appealing place with purpose is the specialty of the design professional trained to work three-dimensionally. And thoughtfully. The thoughtful aspect of decorating cannot be underestimated; it is a vital part of the process whether or not a professional decorator oversees. "A house should grow in the same way an artist's painting grows," says Mario Buatta, a master of charismatic rooms. "A few dabs today, a few more tomorrow," he adds, "and the rest when the spirit moves you. A room that comes together through this process grows along with the people living in it, achieving an ultimately timeless and undecorated look." The undecorated look he refers to is a sense of harmony—a balance of color, texture, and scale.

Color sets a mood. Much has been written about the psychology of color and its powers, but the most persuasive argument for any color remains personal preference. Through the ages color has performed a variety of roles, from alchemist to tranquilizer. (Thomas Jefferson found solace from migraine headaches in a soothing dark green room at Monticello.)

Along with color, texture and scale are essential considerations in the development of a room's character and its comfort level. Texture is derived from furnishings—the upholstery, rugs, artwork, and window dressings. The gloss of polished stone, lacquered woods, and silver accessories suggests formality, while sisal carpet, canvas upholstery, and wicker furniture give just the opposite illusion. Texture and color rely on one another for the integration of a well-designed room. To choose a color without considering the effects of texture would be to leave out a vital step in developing a room's character.

Scale, like color and texture, breathes life into a room as much as the people who enter it. How we live in a space and relate to our surroundings depends upon the scale of the furnishings and the relationship of one object to another. Massive furnishings that dwarf the inhabitants will also intimidate them. Conversely, undersized furniture reduces the chances for comfort and diminishes a room's drama. Scale, then, is the delicate balancing of size and shape, high and low, formal and informal—with comfort and intimacy being the result. How these essentials come together in a room will determine the level of harmony, as in a simple four-poster bed surrounded by white, with little adornment other than a sampler centered between the pillows.

Instead of predictable artwork, this fireplace has a plaster relief hanging on the wall and a gilded mirror standing on the mantel (right). The objects project neoclassical style in harmony with the rest of the living room, which is creamy white.

The symmetry of this bedroom (opposite) was established by the pencil-post bed, its long lines creating a frame of reference for the rest of the furnishings. The writing desk on one side and chair on the other are balanced by a pair of swing-arm lamps and wood frames. In balance, too, are the white walls and bed linens, as well as the bleached wood floor—all of which conspire to make the room orderly and restful. The bedside table serves also as a desk and takes advantage of the adjustable lamp (right).

Black is the common denominator in this dining room (above), with a fireplace intimately involved in the setting. The restrained accessories—an antique basket hung as if it were a painting and a large glass jug filled with tall tulips—balance each other. The dining chairs, thickly upholstered in leather, promise comfort.

One segment of a living room (right) has been carefully orchestrated to invite listening to music. Absolutely nothing upstages the piano, which is centered in the area with a windowed wall on one side and a ceiling-high ficus tree on the other. A large painting is in scale with the dominant piano.

the ultimate
harmony

An English Regency
mirror (above) reflects branches
of spring quince
whose height is similar. The
smaller objects in the
foreground are more diminutive
in scale.

What contributes to
the harmonious balance in this
room (opposite) is the
pairing of objects on the mantel
as well as the pairing
of white and cream. As for
scale, the needlepoint
pillow has ample proportions
similar to the chair's,
and the live bouquet holds its
own next to its
needlepoint counterpoint.

Terms fundamental to interior design—harmony, scale, and color—are, in themselves, abstractions. They only become tangible when a room begins to take form and reflect the tastes of the owner. At that point the three elements ideally merge into a satisfying whole and develop visual personality. The professional designer aids in the developmental stages, seeing to it that the basics get proper attention so that there is an overall harmony in the results.

For New York designers Simone Feldman and Victoria Hagan, harmony, scale, and color are paramount because they put emphasis on a few shapely pieces in predominantly white settings. A generously sized wing chair is a good match for a traditional fireplace. Achieving the balance they do is as much about subtracting as it is about adding objects.

"It takes discipline to keep from adding," says Stephen Mallory, who also subscribes to the lean school of decorating by choosing many shades of white in a room's composition. Each element, then, is emphatic, as is the relationship of one object to another and the ultimate harmony of all, whether the mood is exuberant or serene.

Diverse elements are connected (opposite) with keen attention to scale. The height of the carved chest matches that of the doorway. The dark-framed mirror, matching the chest's tone, hangs at the same level. The pale twig chair, white lamp, and console are underscored by white-stained stripes on the floor.

An oval floral painting (below) is one shapely element in a room based on curves. Not only does it hold the room in balance, its colors relate to the monochromatic scheme created by designers Simone Feldman and Victoria Hagan. Shades of white, cream, and beige blend the walls with the windows and floor.

the subject of color

Identifying with certain colors and spurning others can be rooted in childhood—the pleasant memory of a red chair or the dark recollection of a brown room. Color is a matter of personal taste subject to myriad influences. And to be accepting of certain colors is often a matter of acquired taste. Green, for example, can be hard to warm to if the association with one shade is negative. However, if a new shade is introduced—say, a pale green as the background for floral chintz—the bias may lessen, if not disappear. Such a combination was refined by Mark Hampton in the decoration of a country house.

As he says, "The soft green takes you outdoors and makes the window a frame through which to see

A Connecticut house designed by Sandy Ceppos turned bold. In the living room, red, purple, and turquoise upholstered pieces play off a painted checkerboard floor and spotted-dog table. The designer uses black and white to complement and separate colors. Supporting the graphic design are windows free of curtains and a painting of a pear by Carol Anthony.

the lawn and sky." Conversely, the dark green associated with country porches and shutters has been found to be an energetic indoor color.

For those whose taste runs to even more vigorous colors, black and white can be counted on as they have throughout history. For example, an early seventeenth-century Dutch painting shows a room with black-and-white floor tiles against rich tones of tapestry. Sandy Ceppos is one decorator for whom black and white are catalysts for what she calls "color blocking," a term fashion designers apply to graphic segments of color as in a Mondrian painting. However, Ms. Ceppos tempers her black and white to soften the contrast, a decorating technique that distinguishes her work and makes vivid color schemes easier to live with.

As an art major, Ms. Ceppos learned to mix paints and experiment. Rather than plunging in with great amounts of color, she suggests starting with one colorful piece of furniture or trying out a spirited new color on a small room. "You also have to think about how one color will affect the next room," she says, pointing out the need to create a color plan. Harmony with color, after all, is similar to creating a menu. Consider the ingredients, how they blend, and the resulting taste.

Vermilion walls,
painted in several tones to
achieve a mottled
finish, frame the California
dining room (above)
of Nancy Goslee Power. White
French doors open to
a courtyard with plants that
contribute their
daylight colors to the room. At
night, illuminated by
candles, the walls glow.

Here is an
adventurous approach to color,
with purple casting its
spell over this bedroom (right).
Pale furnishings and
an angled white ceiling
modulate the wall
color, as do the white-shuttered
windows. Designer
Sandy Ceppos advises trying out
strong colors as accents.

Acknowledging the
owner's preference for the clear
colors of her native
Sweden, Mark Hampton chose
apple green for the
walls, sky blue for one sofa, and
a bevy of pinks for
energy (below). White, on the
ceiling, woodwork, and in
the fabric, sharpens the colors.

A sensitive arrangement of colors is reminiscent of the desert, with upholstery in a sand tone and glazed ceramic pots in pale shades (right). A cupboard in its original coat of green harmonizes with the flowering orchid and large-scale floral arrangement.

Hexagonals painted on wide floorboards (below) take their neutral tones from the tweed runner. The pattern begins at the front door and links up with the room beyond, suggesting one continuous space.

The pine ceiling and beams of a remodeled house (opposite below) were purposely lightened—treated with white transparent stain—to be more in tune with the pale surroundings. A burst of seasonal color comes from the tulips. The floor, covered in carpet as neutral as the ceiling, has a slice of color by way of a Scandinavian runner.

Life imitating art: The green, peach, black, and clay (left) respond to an abstract painting by California artist Mary Robertson. Even its margin of white is echoed in the shelf on which the objects are displayed.

The traditional green of country shutters has become a stylish indoor color that appears as fresh as grass (right). Robert K. Lewis used several shades of green as a foil for colors that would likely be found in a summer garden.

The mantel of a torn-down London apartment (below) came with the tenants to their cottage. It houses collections displayed according to color. Slagware, an impure glass collected mainly for its intense shades of purple, is the color focus of the room. The flowers, too, are collected in a single color: yellow for vivid contrast.

This room testifies
to the decorating principle of
using black and white
to calm strong color (above).
Vivid as the wall
color is, it stops short of
piercing due to the
black-and-white patterns and
cooling white trim.
Introducing yet more shades of
green would be a
risky venture if it weren't for
the catalytic effect of
black and white.

When interior
designer Nancy Goslee Power
moved from New
York to California, she adopted
an attitude toward
color that could be called
garden variety. In
fact, every room of her house
has a garden view,
with the living room
commanding the most
lavish one. Its botanical flavor
is strong inside, also.
Green—in plants, fabric,
prints, and the paint
on French doors—accents shell-
pink walls. An umber
velvet sofa and mottled clay-red
desk make up a
palette she calls "forties shades"
in keeping with the
vintage of the house.

the principles
of scale

Contrasts give this city apartment its strong character (above). New York designer Lyn Peterson attributes the end result to a balancing of large pieces (the hutch and table) with smaller objects (the miniature rockers and spindly dining chairs). Architectural elements, she points out, are important to observe.

Scale is to a room what shape is to a garden—essential in the development of balance. That is, the balance between big and small, light and dark, pattern and texture. Achieving successful relationships between these elements is what interior and exterior designers aim to do. The Italian architect Andrea Palladio put forth the principle: "Build in such a manner and with such proportions," he said, "that all the parts together may convey a sweet harmony to the eyes of the beholders."

The analogy between room and garden design also has to do with contrast. Making the elements appropriate to the size of a room is essential to conveying harmony. "More important than what the furniture looks like is the question of scale," says Lyn Peterson of Motif Designs. "It is the judicious balancing of objects that we are after."

The massive fireplace (below) is such a dominant feature of this room that furnishings could easily be dwarfed. The resident, painter Comer Jennings, clipped magazines in pursuit of decorating ideas and developed his own harmony using local crafts. For example, a Georgia quilt draped over the living room table is as strong a presence as the stone fireplace.

A multipurpose
room (above) has little pattern
to distract from the
clarity established by white.
The floor, ceiling,
and walls are in unison, as is the
whitewashed pedestal
table. Freestanding hinged
shutters, close to
ceiling height, were painted a
neutral citrus tone.

The New Orleans design team Ann Holden and Ann Dupuy fashion uncluttered rooms highlighted by well-edited possessions (right). Shades of white provide a soothing background for a hot climate and emphasize interesting silhouettes like that of the tall side table found at a yard sale.

A gold-leaf screen discovered on a fashion designer's business trip to Hong Kong became the main color attraction in her living room (below). Track lights and high-rise windows provide different types of illumination that color the atmosphere according to the time of day. One constant is the room's golden hue imposed by the screen and reinforced by gilded Hepplewhite chairs. Ivory holds the room to a single tone and level of richness.

taming
a
big room

"Humanize the scale," says John Saladino, virtuoso of oversized rooms. An example of his skill is dramatized in this 24-by-40-foot designers' showhouse room. In transforming the space, Saladino displayed his preference for simple geometric forms—chairs and sofas usually of his own design. The room becomes classical in the Saladino manner by virtue of the pure forms, and big becomes intimate by the way he arranges the furnishings. To attempt to duplicate his style would be somewhat like trying to mimic a master chef. However, Saladino points

A large room is composed of distinct areas, two of which are visible here. In order to create intimacy, John Saladino relies on geometric shapes—the rectangular sofa and square, round, and demilune tables. Fabrics by the window are purposely light; those in the center of the room are of a richer teal and cinammon in harmony with the Ushak rug.

A corner in the
Saladino-designed room is part
of one intimate
seating area (above). Its
demilune table holds
a grouping of objects
symmetrically
arranged according to size.

out several design principles which, applied to large rooms, will infuse comfort and intimacy. "You must make the distance between people comfortable for talking," says Saladino.

"Break the room down into distinct zones," says Saladino, who specifies the fireplace as one focus for seating, or what he terms an inglenook. Another zone, the entertainment area, calls for chairs facing a piano or television. A third zone might be for reading, with table, chairs, and appropriate light provided. Each zone, in fact, requires a pool of light for emphasis.

Saladino uses color to identify different zones. Serenity being his goal, the designer—who is also a painter—spreads color in the manner of an impressionist, with subtle gradations. No "agitated" patterns find their way into his rooms; they would interfere with the fine balance and timelessness. Besides, as he puts it, "Today's chintz is tomorrow's dropout."

The fireplace zone, as Saladino sees it, would receive a richer, warmer palette. Areas near windows, where natural light predominates, are complemented by lighter colors and fabrics. The designer's trick of the trade for downplaying, or rendering an upholstered piece anonymous, is to cover it with fabric the color of the carpet. In regard to carpet, Saladino designates the fireplace zone as prime area for a rug, with another in the second seating area. If there were an entertainment area, the floor would be bare for the sake of acoustics as well as visual interest.

By placing a round
table in another section of the
room (left), Saladino
fashions a zone for reading or
letter writing. The
screen and urn are consistent
with the rectangular
and round shapes of the classical
theme.

The room's third
zone (below) is defined by two
sofas, close enough
for conversation and being
warmed by the fire.

small-space strategies

In a dining room cramped for space, a round table is the most efficient choice (left). An antique linen sheet relieves the room of heaviness.

The first floor of a Boston townhouse (right) has been visually stretched well beyond its 500 square feet. Antique porch columns help define three distinct areas.

Most of us have a room that needs to look bigger. Solutions range from architectural devices to paint techniques. Regarding the latter, it is generally agreed that light tones suggest spaciousness and that the lighter the furnishings, the greater the illusion of space. Lightness also refers to using a spare amount of furnishings to emphasize the surrounding ("negative") space.

More ambitious ways to manipulate space go beyond the paintbrush. They involve such architectural elements as platforms, columns, varied ceiling heights, and built-ins. All of these devices were employed in a nineteenth-century rowhouse by Boston designer Peter Wheeler. With only 500 square feet as a first floor but a desire for grandeur, Wheeler approached the area as if it were a stage set. Old porch columns bought at a flea market and left in their weathered state create an entrance pavilion, somewhat like a proscenium. To set the entrance apart from the rest of the room, its ceiling was dropped to eight feet, trimmed with molding and fitted with recessed spotlights. Using the theory that light opens up space, Wheeler painted the room's one old brick wall white. His recommended procedure for covering old brick is a coat of commercial sealer followed by low-luster white applied with a heavy roller. He uses low-luster paint to make the room seem bigger.

The floor is another factor in stretching space. One texture—sisal matting, for example—will have a more enlarging effect than individual area rugs. The same is true for a continuous pattern, as in painted checkerboards. The larger the check, the more white; therefore, the bigger the space will appear.

A room designed by
Keith Irvine (above) seems to
ignore its space
restrictions. The vivid patterns
counterbalance the
effect of a generous amount of
furnishings in a
confined space. What's more,
the room is obviously
designed for comfort and
intimacy—two
qualities exaggerated in such a
small space.

Small rooms with
good proportions have a distinct
advantage (right).
This studio apartment is nearly
square, an ideal shape
by decorating standards. Floor-
to-ceiling mirrors
on either side of the fireplace
magnify the volume of
space. The parchment wallpaper
and blond furnishings
are space amplifiers, also.

odd space
put to good use

The very qualities that make a house unique often pose unique decorating problems. An upstairs dormer, a downstairs alcove, an awkward corner of the kitchen are just some of the quirks that may be charismatic on one hand and baffling on the other. Decorating the odd space is often a matter of theatrics—creating a stage for showing off art objects— or a more practical consideration such as carving a niche for a workshop or office. If the space is more luxury than necessity, liberties can be taken with its use. As an example, the stairway landing of an older home could have enough room for a bookshelf or cupboard and serve as a miniature library for a home with a surplus of books. A wide hall that happens to have a window might lend itself to a window seat. The same applies to dormers, often too narrow for anything other than a seat or perhaps a small dressing table. By process of elimination, after taking inventory of all the necessary rooms, one can decide what is needed after all. The fact is, the odd space can be a dividend, an extra added attraction.

An entrance hall with room under the stairwell (above) has both a table for seasonal displays of flowers and a wallpapered French screen concealing a rack of out-of-season clothes. The extra-wide windowsill, characteristic of older houses, serves as a display shelf.

The double-height
entryway (left) has enough
vertical space for a
sizable chandelier, but modest
floor space. A mirror
reflects the light background
and is a useful
accessory to the chest,
convenient for
sundries.

The odd room in a
house became office space
(left). Country
antiques, collected for their
simplicity, are used
instead of more conventional
office furniture.
And in place of a diploma
or other framed
credentials, a 19th-century
English sampler
hangs over the work table.

The far end of a narrow kitchen (opposite) benefits from multiple windows and transparent door. A round table proved to be the most accommodating shape for the sunny, albeit awkward space in which four can sit comfortably. A slender standard rose stands by one wall, a natural form of decoration that replaces artwork.

An alcove (above left) that could easily be thought of as quaint but useless has been transformed into a guest nook or reading corner. A banquette built in to fit the space precisely has a ledge in lieu of an end table. The novel window and vaulted ceiling give the area a lift.

The windowed corner of an old house (above) turns into a stage for a folk art horse whose proportions seem to be custom-made for the odd space. A harmonious arrangement of objects can be appreciated for their individual silhouettes backlit by the window.

Nancy Goslee Power
fills the ample corners of her
living room with
versatile tables on either end of
the sofa. A Regency
pedestal table (right), a classic
once used behind
sofas, serves as a library table
illuminated by the
large window and the corner
lamp. The opposite
corner has a round table covered
with a floor-length
cloth; it conceals stacks of
decorating magazines
and the family television set
housed on a cart—
"An old New York apartment
trick," says Ms.
Power of the hidden space.

corners: conscious choices

The corner of a
young boy's bedroom (right) has
a sophisticated mix
of an antique chest with a
collector's toy airplane.

Time was when the corner represented a hiding place; it got hardly any respect as a room's extra dimension, let alone as a place to use creatively. Designers, though wise to the ways of rendering corners passive or active, can make them work to a room's advantage. At times that may mean treating a corner as if it weren't even there.

Such was the case when Boston designer William Hodgins took on a "peculiar" floor plan in a 1920s house. When two rooms were combined into one long, narrow living room, the original off-center fireplace posed a decorating problem: how to arrange the furniture to create intimacy with focus on the fireplace. "It seemed to make the area near the fireplace warmer and friendlier to put the sofa across the corner," says Hodgins. The consequence of that solution was a different problem: how to treat the resulting empty space behind the sofa. Hodgins introduced a screen to fill in the area decorously.

Nancy Goslee Power's California living room included two nice, big, fat corners. Her solution to corners without purpose was to fill them with tables.

The 18th-century
French screen (below) decorates
a corner left useless
when William Hodgins angled
the sofa in an oddly
shaped living room. Not only
does the screen fill a
void, its scenery envelops the
conversation area.

double-duty design

What could pass as a modernist's painting or freestanding wall is actually a storage unit (above) without exterior hardware that might reveal its identity. Texas bluebonnets inspired its color.

The "wall" (opposite), fitted with interior hinges, opens to reveal more than 700 books, records, and compact discs. A thicker center shelf adds support to the outer walls.

Storage, like money, is rarely abundant enough. To solve this perennial problem, designers and architects call on their inventiveness, often coming up with more than one solution—the unit that holds audio equipment also divides the room; the stairway that serves as a sculptural element also ascends to a loft. Strategies like these were applied by Houston, Texas, architect Carlos Jimenez in his 480-square-foot house. Through the spare use of furnishings, with emphasis on versatility and color, Jimenez organized

and energized the compact space. Referring to color as comforting and sensuous, he exploited those qualities with an intensely blue freestanding wall that evokes images of a minimalist painting. Yet the wall is highly functional—hundreds of music tapes and books are housed inside. Proof of its design success is its dual function, first as a substantial room divider that bestows privacy on the dining and living areas, and second as an efficient storage unit. And the wall has the bonus of being an aesthetic contribution to every angle of the room.

51

A sitting room
is particularly amenable to
overnight guests who
can recline on the antique
daybed, a space-
saving alternative to the
convertible sofa.

a little
private
space

Community space and private space are the two vital components of a home. Parents need a separation from children and adults from each other, and ideally, separate rooms can be designated for the pursuit of privacy. However, if individual rooms are simply not available, resourcefulness can always be employed. A single piece of furniture, in fact, can symbolize privacy. A chaise, dressing table, or wing chair has that capability if it is situated in a remote spot. The chest of drawers is a traditional one-person furnishing. Designed to be autonomous, the chest is a personal repository. Then there is the writing desk, the quintessential private space. "Everyone should have a writing desk, secretary, or chest of drawers where you can have all your treasures," says designer Robert K. Lewis, who sees the bedroom the likely place to house such pieces.

Out of the bedroom
in a city apartment (left), room
was carved for
privacy. Corner windows
allowed space for a
luxurious silver-leaf chaise, next
to which an Ionic
capital acts as a table. The view
can be shared from
the writing desk, positioned
against one wall.

A grand gesture
(above) is appropriate for a
master bedroom of
luxurious proportions. New
York designer Robert
K. Lewis treated the room to
heirloom designs,
with particular flourish in
regard to a writing
desk. He chose a Chippendale
secretary, whose desk
holds all the accoutrements for
daily journal keeping
or letter writing.

55

One piece of
furniture can fulfill a variety of
needs (left). The
Scandinavian-style secretary
placed against a living
room wall presents itself as a
curio cabinet and
writing desk with intimate
seating for two.

The bedroom
endowed with a chaise (below)
has the innate luxury
of a sitting area. Because of the
surplus space here,
one section has been designated
as a private corner for
reading and watching television.
The television is
housed in the painted armoire
which is angled in its
corner so that it is also visible
from the bed.

The balcony in the
upper reaches of a lake house is
furnished to be both
an escape and a vantage point
(opposite). Secluded
from other rooms, the balcony
has all the requisites
for a reading corner, plus the
bonus of natural light
and extensive views. Purely
black and white,
down to the stained checkerboard floor, the area
is as graphic as the crossword
puzzles completed there.

CHAPTER TWO

THE ELEMENTS

walls, windows, floors, and ceilings

Our home environment speaks for our life. This personal communication has less to do with the verbal and more to do with the physical elements—the walls, windows, architectural features, floors, and ceilings. How we respond to each of these elements has something significant to say about us, whether our taste runs to minimalism—a person of few words, perhaps—or to the abundance of an extrovert.

The character of a room depends on how its basic elements are shaped. Whether the walls are quietly pristine or busy with pattern is revealing: The pristine implies a fondness for order, while busy walls send a message of exuberance, perhaps a love of texture and color. The point is, walls speak.

Awareness helps guide our choices. Think about how windows affect a room. Do they provide the appropriate amount of light, requiring only decorative curtains? Or might they need to be draped to dim the light flooding into a room? Of course, a window that overlooks a garden may need no curtain to shade the view.

Floors, too, can communicate. They have been known to creak or, when luxuriously carpeted, cause a hush. The way a floor presents itself—plain, polished, painted, tiled, or carpeted—contributes importantly to the room's comfort and aesthetic.

Ceilings are more than uplifting. They can be colorful, textural, fanciful, or just plain. With the help of electric fixtures or skylights, ceilings become vital sources of light. The point is not to take any part of a room for granted—not even the ceiling.

Elements rely on one another for unity. The walls, windows, floors, and ceilings must be compatible in color, texture, and scale. In cases where the given architectural elements prevent unity, they don't have to be accepted meekly. Windows can be enlarged visually if not structurally; the same applies to stairways, doors, floors, and ceilings. In fact, newly installed architectural features—a distinctive stair railing and newel post, elaborate molding, or a column or two—can become as integral to a room as good bones are to a face. And no one will ever know they weren't part of the original structure.

The elements can always be altered. One vivid description of such sleight of hand is in Gene Fowler's *Good Night, Sweet Prince*, a book about actor John Barrymore and his unusual Greenwich Village apartment. "After he had surfaced the walls with Chinese gold," the author recounts, "Barrymore lighted church candles and spent many hours smoke-smudging the walls and furniture. It was this aging of his retreat that caused him to refer to it as the Alchemist's Corner."

walls
set a stage

A small city
apartment had its walls, floor,
and ceiling
transformed with multiple
layers of brown paint,
topped with a mirrorlike glaze
(above). The illusion
is that of a fine leather trunk.

From the earliest dwellings to modern-day houses, walls act like blank slates for their inhabitants. Cave dwellers expressed feelings through pictograms; seventeenth-century aristocrats paneled walls in fine wood and added grand painted effects with graining or marbling; twentieth-century sophisticates hand-paint walls to mimic exquisitely distressed relics.

The legacy includes artwork, without which walls—and those who live within them—would be deprived. So important was artwork to the completeness of rooms that the famous nineteenth-century household guide, *American Woman's Home*, told readers to set aside twenty percent of the budget just for pictures. Along with art, authors Harriet Beecher Stowe and her sister, Catherine, listed wallpaper and border among decorating's top priorities.

A century later, the decorating authority Dorothy Draper called attention to the color of walls in no uncertain terms: "There should never be any doubt about what your color has to say. It may be lemon-yellow, watermelon-pink, chocolate-brown, or anything you like, just as long as it knows its own mind. Muddy walls are nothing but a blight." A level of confidence, or lack of it, is always communicated by walls—through their color, quality

of paintwork, style of covering, and content of artwork.

Painted techniques, in themselves artwork, can transform walls—and ultimately rooms—as if by magic. Marbling, stipling, dragging, and all the other decorative treatments passed down through the ages continue to inspire painters determined to change ordinary walls by sleight of hand. For decorator George Constant, the desired image was the inside of a ship—just the opposite of the anonymous high-rise apartment he was commissioned to decorate. Staring out at the Statue of Liberty from the square white living room, the designer found his inspiration in its nautical context and weather-worn surface. Constant chose to create an enveloping space, with all the surfaces covered in the same rich, dark paint. By treating all the surfaces of the room as one, he created a total environment. "A sim-

ple concept," he says—and one that could also be accomplished with wallpaper.

Covering surfaces with paper tends to be less intricate than applying decorative paint techniques. That process requires meticulous preparation of the walls and artful handwork to achieve effects. Then there is the finishing or glazing necessary to give the surface a polish. With wallpaper, the coverage is more predictable and likely to be less expensive.

Adding details to plain walls can also be accomplished with architectural elements purchased from lumber yards or mail order sources. Wainscoting, for example, can be attached to the lower portion of walls in any room, including the bath. For the upper part of walls, choices include cornices, crown moldings, or features in keeping with others in the room. Suitability is, after all, key to any embellishment of walls.

Decorative paint techniques were employed in a showcase kitchen (left) to impart old-world flavor. Sponging and rubbing transformed cabinets and even the stove hood; limestone tiles in a harlequin pattern blend with the stonelike wall color. Frosted glass on the cabinets adds luster and dimension, as does the mirrored backsplash.

Sponge-painted walls in pale pink (below) are set off by delftware. The crisp, cool color of the pottery is repeated as a doorway border. New York designer Richard Lowell Neas orchestrated freehand squiggles and comb-painted stripes in a blue-and-white motif that also creates borders around the windows.

The spirit of New Mexico pervades this bedroom (opposite) with walls the shade of midnight. The strength of the wall color is heightened by flat paint which, unlike gloss, forgives surface flaws. Luminous color intensifies other colors, as in the Gerber daisies and primitive figure displayed on the ledge of an interior window. A contrasting pale tone surrounds the cutout and filters light into the room.

The Georgia lake
house of artist Comer Jennings
sports a wall flag he
made of slats, baling wire, a
wood square, and
stenciled stars (right). Its stripes
are a pleasing contrast
to the vertical wallboards.

The walls of this
1920s kitchen incorporate a
bench and high shelf
(below). Designer Leslie Allen
whitened everything so the
emphasis would be
shifted to a plate collection and
her shapely chairs.

Painting dark
tongue-and-groove paneling a
clean white put fresh
perspective on a weekend house
(above). The
inexpensive yet resourceful
decorating includes
store-bought swags of dotted
swiss and frames
from the attic minus pictures.
The stenciled checks
around the fireplace repeat the
square theme of the
frames and are painted the color
of light wood.

A small room (left)
will always benefit from white
walls and shutters. As
with the furnishings, the
wall treatment is
geometric, with related pictures
all hung at eye level.

Walls shaped by a steeply pitched roof, as in an attic conversion, pose a unique challenge. In this instance, the A-shaped paneled ceiling adds dimension to the walls and is painted the same shade for continuity. The symmetry of three windows was repeated with triple prints hung in a row.

A room with heavy wood molding gets relief from striped wallpaper (below), as well as a white ceiling. Both the pattern of the paper and the expanse of white complement the room's other patterns and abundant color—green being the one picked out for the stripe. Another form of white, the cream-toned curtains contribute to the decorative influence of the walls.

Evocative of a
vigorous English garden, this
room is lavished with
cabbage roses, from the walls to
the curtains (left).
The mirror, as ornate as the
flowers are colorful,
is a sign of sure-handed
decorating.

The walls of a
dining room by Mark
Hampton (below) are
distinctive for their melon color
and ribbon-motif
border. Edging the upper part
of the room as it does,
the border suggests a fanciful
molding. The design
is by Swedish artist Carl Larsson.
Another overhead decoration,
also from Sweden, is
the crystal and candle
chandelier.

A stairway and upper landing turn scenic in the tradition of those 18th-century itinerant muralists who brought the outside in. This landscape evokes folk art paintings, with the trees in the foreground creating an illusion of intimacy like that of a diorama. The mural, hand-drawn and then painted in acrylic, was executed by the New York firm of Marshall/Schule.

window dressing

A whimsical
approach to window dressing is
applied with paint
around a window that didn't
require covering for
privacy (right). Artist Virginia
Teichner created
a checkerboard curtain draped
at the sides, complete
with brackets, pole, and tie-
backs.

Windows, focal points from both inside and out, are likely candidates for decorative techniques. A case could also be made for leaving windows bare, especially those with architectural interest. Many decorators, in fact, advocate naked windows, particularly if views are more important than privacy. On the other hand, houses encumbered with awkward windows usually benefit from inventive decoration.

Dormer windows, with their deep recesses, present a unique decorating challenge. They can be viewed as charming niches and treated accordingly, with pleated shades or sheer fabric attached to the top and bottom. If the recess of the window creates a

deep enough ledge, potted flowers can be arranged like an indoor window box. That leaves the upper part available for an informal swag, with one length of soft fabric folded over a rod so that the sides hang evenly and the center portion dips down.

Another option somewhere between bare windows and those with

covering is the painted variety. The cottage with chipped mullions and sills can be vastly improved with the application of bright color in lieu of curtains. More ambitious decorative techniques can transform windows from the common variety into fanciful apertures with elaborate valances and yards of fabric.

The plaster walls
and timbers of a two-hundred-
year-old house are
most evident at its windows
(left). To cover them
entirely would be to block out
their essential charm.
The striped swag, coordinated
with slipcovers, offers
minimal coverage with a degree
cf softness and
provides a refreshing change in
summer.

The pleated fabric
shade (above) screens out the
sun partially or
entirely depending on whether a
garden view is
desired. As a decorative
element, the shade's
stripe motif unifies it with
the walls.

The symmetry and
light in an architect's studio
(right) are magnified
by multiple glass squares. Thin-
slatted blinds calm
the abundant sunshine, yet have
a transparent quality.

A chaise, angled in front of a California garden, has the advantage of natural light for the reader (below). Rather than drape the windows, the owner chose vertical metal blinds that resemble tight pleats when open. Fastened to a ceiling track, the custom, neutral-toned blinds extend to the floor in the manner of tailored draperies. When drawn, the blinds become a wall of soft color and texture.

The window seat is
enfolded with triple-layered
theater-style curtains
(above). Sheer fabric is gathered
up in scallops and
placed closest to the window.
Slightly heavier
fabric hangs to the floor, caught
up on either side to
frame the window seat or drawn
for a more formal
effect.

The fashion for
sheer curtains increases with our
growing desire for
more natural light. The latest
generation of
synthetic fabrics also contributes
to the high quality
and easy care of sheer curtains.
One diaphanous panel
(opposite) is enough to drape
a tall window, with
the fabric gathered around a
brass rosette that
matches the rod's finials.

French doors,
graceful in themselves, don't
necessarily need
coverage unless privacy is
required. The
bedroom is one of those
instances (above).
Luxuriously long cotton duck
curtains were hung
from iron rods instead of the
traditional wood
poles. When the curtains are
pulled back, the doors
are framed in soft fabric.

A guest bathroom
(right) has both the advantage
of a window and
the need for some privacy.
A shade or
conventional curtains would
have been acceptable
options, but New York interior
designer Mariette
Himes Gomez chose to
improvise. She
looped antique linen squares
over a rod to create
sheer, angled curtains.

A pair of windows
(right) is treated as one, with
a single rod attached
just under the molding. English
lace, complete with
holes for the rod, covers the
span of the windows,
leaving the bottom portion bare.
The windowsill,
convenient to the kitchen
counter, has space for
pots of herbs that grow under
the zigzag hem.

An impressive
chandelier (opposite) would
be less so if its
background was a fussy
window treatment.
Sheer curtains, drawn back at
the lowest pane, bring
tranquility to the setting.

Finials (right) on the ends of wood poles have handpainted relief designs that evoke planting fields. The pole is an artistic expression, also, with painted flowers drawn as a continuation of some of those in the curtain.

Extra-large poles (below) contribute to the woodsy atmosphere of a paneled room where natural textures predominate. A nubby fabric of linen and cotton makes up the pinch-pleat curtains that hang from the ceiling molding to the floor.

Ready-made curtains (far right) have zigzag edges and embroidered medallions that would ordinarily be associated with custom work. Long enough to drip fashionably on the floor, the panels are used on the windows and French doors alike. They were dyed a soft peach and hung from brass rods, with starfish finials (opposite above) as punctuation.

Striped valances over plain curtains give a simple unity to the traditional windows in a Colonial house (right). In this room, the valances provide a decorative cap to windows that have no ornamentation. Their warm stripe corresponds with the similarly colored molding, wallpaper, and chair covering.

Deeply recessed windows (below) are purposely left bare for emphasis. With an absence of curtains, valances have strong impact, particularly these striped varieties. They call immediate attention to the windows, which, if left totally bare, would become upstaged by the floral prints and imposing coffee table.

An unusually long
window (left) is dramatized by
the striped swag that
borders the top and falls
halfway down each
side. Another embellishment is
the scalloped frieze
painted in colors of the
window's fabric and
coordinated with the walls
and the upholstery.

A matching valance
and curtains (left) set the
stage for a curvaceous
piece of furniture. With just
one window in a
narrow space, the floor-to-
ceiling treatment and
minimal pattern give the room
more fullness.

A bay of windows (right) is thoroughly dressed with tie-back curtains and a deep valance. Shutters screen out any intrusion to this niche, which is both a window seat and a bed. The bed skirt is a gathering of folds that matches the valance.

This interior place to commune with nature (below) is nestled within the framework of vintage windows. The boxed cushion, covered in a fabric evocative of the garden, ensures a comfortable seat near the antique birdcage.

A house built in 1826 had Gothic windows among its charms (opposite). Boston designer William Hodgins amplified the charm of matching dormer windows by adding window seats to a bedroom's architecture. The windows themselves were dressed in stage-curtain fashion with crisp cotton fabric hung on a rod curved to comply with the arch. A hidden cord pulls the curtain back on either side. The lower level sheer curtain, called a brisbee, forms a cloudlike cover.

architectural
elements

Certain features of a room deserve to be played up; they are often sources of pride. Those features can be inherent or integral parts of the architecture, such as a fireplace or window. Or they can be mobile added attractions such as columns, sculpture, or artwork.

The fireplace is perhaps the most obvious focal point; it's usually center stage. Playing up that feature is one of the most fundamental aspects of decorating: Use the mantel as a shelf for displaying important objects, reserve the area above it for a significant painting, train light on the subject, or arrange seating to establish a close relationship with it.

What will provide a focus in a room without such a dominant feature? Enter the world of architectural elements, the moldings, mantels, and columns that many rooms never had in the first place, but inherited at

A new house was
infused with focal points to
make its large, bland
rooms more gracious. Georgia
designer Dan Carithers
found ready-made architectural
trimmings of
molded polyurethane and had
them installed as
the house was being built. The
moldings, whose details
were picked out in white, give
the room a classical air.

a later stage. In other words, some focal points may be created in the process of a room's evolution. Those elements, like actual furnishings, can be shopped for. Sources may vary from antiques markets to demolition sites where fragments from old buildings are considered ornaments worthy of saving. In fact, many corbels and columns have been transferred from commercial buildings to residences in need of ornamentation. Reproductions of architectural ornaments are also readily available through mail order catalogs and stores that specialize in unique accessories.

The success of a focal point has as much to do with the positioning of the object as it does with the object itself. Wall niches were made to attract attention; they are display cases whose shelves typically graduate from low to eye level so that the objects displayed can be appreciated from sitting or standing positions. The boundaries for positioning paintings are less structured. Walls are open planes, so the decision becomes whether to give one painting prominence on the wall, while avoiding glare from a window, or to arrange a series of pictures so the emphasis is on the group rather than the individual. That's where the pride of ownership comes into play.

Molded polyurethane trim duplicates traditional wood and plasterwork. In this room (left), the 15-foot-high tray ceiling was given distinction with a grid of beams; the windows have curved moldings that "stretch the scale," according to designer Dan Carithers.

An old house inside the new one (below) sits on a table behind the sofa. The English 19th-century dollhouse is another focal point and imparts authentic history. Framed by French doors, the antique is naturally lit by day and is visible from every part of the room.

A new house devoid of architectural details made the transition to classical style with a number of ready-made moldings. The boxlike dining room (opposite) received sunburst arches over the windows, elements that seem to increase the room's height. Cornice moldings were added to marry the walls with the window arches.

A house is in the details (this page). Connecticut architects Beinfield Wagner & Associates created an echo of their exterior design with miniaturized elements that are begun on the first level and then repeated from level to level. The house, therefore, has surprise awaiting at each landing. The first is a banister, with the shape of the house itself instead of the customary newel post. The second and third walkways incorporate the house detail with railings whose color makes even more of the ornamentation. A catwalk bridge at the top level extends to a small balcony and the outside, which is referred to all along.

Embellishing a fireplace opening (opposite) with a period mantel whose details are repeated in the cornice and window molding is a typical design tactic. Here it not only adds authenticity to the room, but its continuous light green hue also ties the fireplace to the windows.

paying attention
to floors

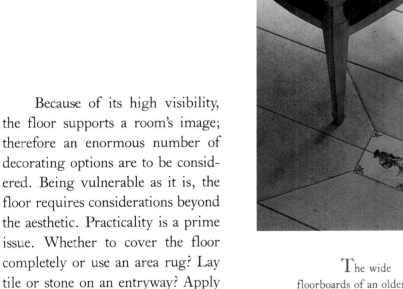

The wide
floorboards of an older house
(above and opposite)
were sanded, then rubbed with
white paint to make
them pale. Believable tiles are
actually painted on
the wood by an artist inspired
by Dutch designs. A
shiny finish was applied to make
the tiles appear
glazed, like the real thing.

Because of its high visibility, the floor supports a room's image; therefore an enormous number of decorating options are to be considered. Being vulnerable as it is, the floor requires considerations beyond the aesthetic. Practicality is a prime issue. Whether to cover the floor completely or use an area rug? Lay tile or stone on an entryway? Apply decorative paint techniques or sand and polish? Cover the steps or not?

What to do about steps—a universal dilemma—depends on the surroundings, of course. "If stair risers are one of the first things you see when walking into a hall, you can't leave them bare," says New York decorator Carolyn Gutilla. A positive first impression is guaranteed if the risers are decorated with stencils or covered with a colorful runner. As for steps integrated in rooms with mostly bare floors, the choice to leave them bare may be the smartest.

Any decision regarding floors

should be based on the size of the room, its purpose, and the style of the house. Interior designers generally agree that a confined space benefits from either a bare floor or a totally covered one—as opposed to bringing in a small area rug, which would chop up the limited space. Sisal or

coir matting often appears in professionally decorated rooms because it gives a feeling of spaciousness while offering a subtle overall texture. What's more, sisal can be laid with invisible binding as a large area rug so that it appears to cover the entire floor. The effect is similar to that of a uniformly finished wood floor. And like a bare wood floor, sisal can be painted or stenciled.

The floor is, in fact, a prime candidate for stenciling and faux paint techniques. Artists specializing in decorative painting can transform a plain floor into one that appears tiled, marbled, inlaid, or a composite of techniques. Some floors lend themselves particularly well to superimposed design. As an example, the wide floorboards typical of century-old houses are often found in a decrepit state. Applying paint in a thin coat after sanding, then quickly rubbing it off, allows the old grain to show through, creating an image that could spark modern-day poetry.

Attention lavished on the floor and walls of an entry hall (left) reflects two decorative techniques with paint. The art of faux painting creates a floor that appears to be composed of inlay and marble. Another faux technique, applied to the walls, imitates limestone. Both contribute to the grand illusion of decorator Gary Crain's New York apartment. In concert, the walls and floor are an appropriately rich-looking background for the George III console.

The wide floorboards of a vintage country house masquerade as inlay of a rustic variety (opposite). Knotted pine octagonals, stenciled against white paint, have green squares linking them and giving a sense of depth. The floor's pale wood and low luster correspond to the reproduction 1840s furnishings. Connecticut designer Beverly Ellsley emphasized the floor with turquoise molding.

The architecture of
Hugh Newell Jacobsen
(opposite) integrates
strong materials evocative of the
surrounding
countryside. Flat stone, like that
of a terrace, paves the
long corridor of an entryway,
whose adjacent floor
is natural wood.

Natural wood, laid
on the diagonal, stretches the
dimensions of a
compact library (above). Since
the floor is bleached,
it tends to fade into the
background, allowing
the diagonal lines of the rug to
be the predominant
pattern.

The floor in front of
a fireplace (left) appears to be
natural wood but is
actually a flat-woven tweed. Its
subtle texture
provides just enough cushion to
anchor the furniture
and provide warmth underfoot.
Incorporated in the
carpet's weave is the blue-gray
tone which colors the
walls.

The unpretentious
bedroom of a period house
(below) has its
windows bare and its floor
essentially covered
with basic grass matting.
A small, richly
patterned rug is layered on top,
designating the sitting
area by the fireplace.

The conversation
area in a living room (opposite)
receives geometric
pattern and rose color from the
rug. Its coverage is
close to being complete;
however, there is a
margin of wood floor on the
outskirts of the room
and under the sofa. Therefore,
the rug's border lines
up with the skirt of the sofa.

In a light-filled
sunroom, the rug dominates
with strong support
from stripes (left) and clarity
from white. Such a
riotous pattern has the energy of
a profusely blooming
garden made more emphatic by
the white-painted
floorboards.

Floor and walls of
the same tone (above) make a
small box of a room
seem bigger. Sisal covers the
entire floor in a warm
tan, similar to that of the
furniture. One
liberty taken with the
monochromatic
theme is turquoise upholstery
set off by a man-made
zebra rug of jungle stripes.

A small landing
(right) has a runner that is
interrupted and then
continued up the next flight of
stairs. The first riser,
in unison with the woodwork, is
painted rather than
carpeted as the rest are.

The dark wood steps
of a cottage (below) are
brightened by an
improvised runner, actually
hooked chair pads.
The floral designs, as identical
as the steps, cover
enough to accommodate two
feet. The pads are
securely fastened with
carpet tacks.

The entry-hall
pavilion of a residence by
architect Hugh
Newell Jacobsen (opposite) has a
stairwell that might as
well be sculpture. Linear from
the banister to the
underside of the steps, the area
has a combination of
materials both practical and
aesthetic. The
entrance is paved in stone, and
the steps cushioned
with sturdy, sand-colored tight-
woven carpet.

Washington
decorator Mary Douglas
Drysdale took sisal a
step beyond convention by
applying stencil
designs as a running border.
The stylized motif
(above), a strong contrast on the
natural matting, is as
black as the slate floor of the
entrance to this
showcase house.

options
for ceilings

If a ceiling's importance were to be measured in terms of square footage, it would top every other interior element. And because of its volume, the ceiling plays a major role, be it passive or active, in setting the style of a room. A flat, plain white surface would qualify as passive or neutral—important nonetheless as it directs one to decorative elements at eye level. The ceiling that plays a more active role has beams, height variations, or possibly curves and assorted angles. Such ceilings either reinforce or establish the mood of a room.

The somewhat square room with a flat ceiling is a prime candidate for decorative attention. This can range from molding and cornices that create architectural distinction to paint or wallpaper that create illusions of bigger space. If the objective is to make a ceiling look higher, for example, lighter colors would be the best choice. If the intent is to make a ceiling look lower, its color would be a darker shade than the walls.

The ceiling is receptive to all manner of illusions, many of which can be painted. The bedroom may be turned into a night sky; the dining room into an arbor with a trellis of ivy trailing down the walls. Trompe l'oeil illusions of architectural interest can also be added to imitate moldings or give dimension to those already there. Architectural details

can also be introduced.

Ceilings of the more aggressive type, say, the dark, heavy-beamed variety associated with paneled libraries or mountain houses, may need to be subdued. In this case, beams recede if they are painted a light tone along with the ceiling. On the other hand, beams lend great interest to a room if they are in harmony with the furnishings.

Another type of complement is the fabric-covered ceiling based on the tent. This is particularly effective for ceilings that need lowering, though another way is to install a lower, false ceiling.

A simpler way to use fabric on the ceiling would be to upholster it in the same manner as on walls, that is, seaming lengths of material together and stapling them on with or without padding underneath. Lower ceilings often lend themselves to this treatment. The point is, no matter what its height, the ceiling is a vital dimension in every room's style.

The ceiling functions as a utility center over a kitchen work surface. It houses task lighting focused on the cooking island. An iron rack with movable hooks holds everyday pots, with clusters of garlic and peppers in easy reach of the cook.

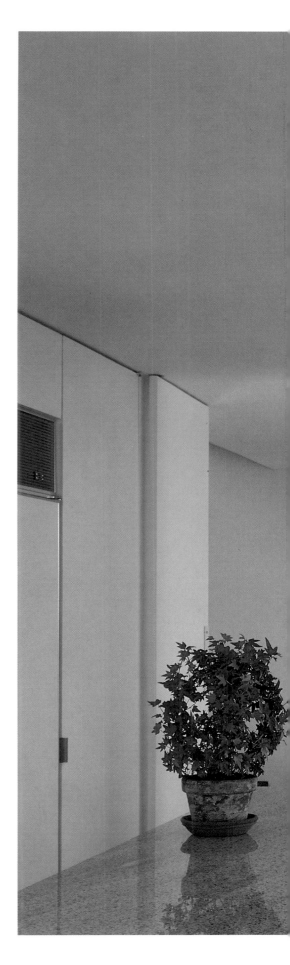

Customs House in Cornwall, England, became a stencil showcase for artist Lyn Le Grice, who works unconventionally with spray paint to achieve luminous colors and bold designs. She used the grape motif in the dining room (left) to stencil an arbor replete with these ancient symbols of feasting. The window shade, too, has been stenciled, as have the chairs and napkins.

Ms. Le Grice achieves a dappled quality to her stencils by layering colors, as in the sky of this nursery (opposite). The firmament she created lights up a unique canopy ceiling original to the early 18th-century English house.

The kitchen and
family room addition to an old
barn (left) has aged
beams to maintain the rustic
spirit. To counteract
the dark rafters, white is used
in between, with
recessed spots pouring light on
the entire area.

When walls are
colored as this is (below), the
ceiling will appear
higher if it is white. In this case
a beam serving no
aesthetic purpose is diminished
by being the same
white as the ceiling.

In a two-story living
room (opposite), the vaulted
ceiling is colored as if
it were sky. Reminiscent of
traditional verandahs
with blue ceilings, this has
narrow paneling
instead of rafters. The railing
with its vertical strips
is another porch-inspired
feature.

A porchlike
atmosphere pervades the second
story of a cottage
(above) with its pitched ceiling
and rafters. And like
a summer porch, the boards and
beams are painted
white. The result is an openness
with no loss of
architectural interest. In fact,
the horizontal and vertical
lines strengthen the design.

The upstairs library
of a weekend house in the
mountains was kept as
light as the rest of the rooms
(opposite). An
important ingredient is the
ceiling—pine panels
that were given a thin coat of
white to match the
texture and lightness of the
walls. Recessed spots
provide ample overhead light.

CHAPTER THREE

THE DETAILS

where style comes into play

"God is in the details," said architect Mies van der Rohe. While he was addressing the subject of restraint in design, his statement has been placed in a wide variety of contexts. A universal truth, the phrase applies to all the arts and here, specifically, to decorating.

It is in the details that a room becomes greater than the sum of its parts. The most accessible, the most malleable, the most personal, the most exciting part of designing a room, the details give us the greatest satisfaction. They are the touchstones of our lives, those objects that singly and together represent us. They are tactile—the fabric that covers a sofa, the cool crystal vase that holds summer flowers. They are sentimental—the sterling frames of family photographs, the needlework pillow in the curve of a favorite reading chair. They are familiar—Mother's mirror that has hung in the hall for years, a child's watercolor on the bedroom wall. Details can be both timeless and transitional, changing with the family and with the seasons.

Design professionals like Robert K. Lewis, for example, are astute observers of details, attentive to the subtle as well as the obvious. One of the essentials in Mr. Lewis's practice is the inclusion of end tables, which, because of his traditional bent, are usually antique. "You have to have a surface adjacent to the sofa," he insists, "and the height of the table depends on the arm of the sofa. Most antiques tend to be higher than the usual sofa arm." Though Mr. Lewis has no objections to a slightly higher end table, he has been known to substitute an antique tea table for the newer generation coffee table. In fact, breaking the rules may sometimes be exactly the way to proceed.

Balance plays an important role when paying attention to detail. Will a chintz skirt on a dressing table be too busy in a bedroom with printed wallpaper? Can a round table in a small dining room enhance the sense of space? Achieving a delicate balance is something Georgina Fairholme perfects again and again in her New York design practice. Ms. Fairholme may choose to start at the windows with curtains she prefers to line with "something pretty." Or she may finish a library bookshelf with molding or a scalloped wallpaper border.

Ultimately, attention to details is what conveys personality in a room. But, of the urge to decorate lavishly, Georgina Fairholme is adamant: "You have to know when to stop."

entries: lasting first impressions

One well-endowed entry (left) has French doors with a fanlight, an elegant combination repeated in the adjoining room. More architectural detail was introduced with the addition of a door frame and pediment from an older structure. Lightness prevails, from the creamy walls and ceiling to the pale, stenciled floor.

A multipaned front door (opposite) lights the entrance and gives it a view of the landscape as well as arriving guests. Space allows for an ideal situation: a pair of mirrors and consoles.

Behind every front door lurks an area that poses a special decorating challenge. Depending on the architecture of the building, an entrance may be inherently gracious or, at the worst, devoid of any positive qualities at all. The ideal entry would have the luxury of space, enough to allow more than two people stretching room. And it would have ample light, overhead as well as on the wall, and a mirror for reasons of vanity (a quick look upon arriving or leaving).

There would be a closet just for guests, an attractive table to hold flowers keys, and mail, and space to display artwork. The handsome, practical floor would be tiled, carpeted, or left bare and polished. And, as is the case in some fine old buildings, there would be architectural details in the form of columns or molding. For the entrance hall devoid of any such amenities, there are ideas to be gleaned from those who have met this decorating challenge successfully.

115

A fashion designer's entrance hall (right) reveals her taste for elegant materials and subdued colors. Reflected in the circular mirror is a 19th-century Italian head elevated with books. New York designer Stephen Mallory created the setting to suggest an Italian palazzo. He installed limestone tile floors and an entrance door painted to resemble steel and bronze.

A glass-topped iron console (right) acts as a miniature gallery, displaying memorabilia and three architectural prints that lean informally rather than hang. The vacant space underneath allows for an Indian basket, a catchall for newspapers, magazines, and packages to be mailed.

A house celebrates itself in a mural (this page). Rather than hanging an anonymous wallpaper pattern, the owner commissioned a muralist whose work recalled that of 19th-century itinerant artist Rufus Porter. The scenery is true to life—a depiction of the actual house and farm including the family's dogs and chickens. The dominant green in the painting also colors the chair rail and the stenciled floor diamonds.

117

slipcovers: infinite chic

The vogue for slipcovers has its roots in the middle ages when furniture was built to travel. Common benches, often part of the luggage, metamorphosed into richly embroidered seats. By the eighteenth century, it became a summer custom to cover furniture with embroidered cotton and to use the same material as replacement for heavy draperies.

Much like summer wardrobes which tend to be fresh looking and easy fitting, slipcovers are furniture's change of clothes. While they do provide a welcome decorative transition, slipcovers also fulfill a practical need. A bonus of using slipcovers is that the longevity of upholstered furniture increases. Obviously the wear and tear diminishes when original fabric gets covered for a portion of the year. Given the cost of re-upholstery, the cover has become a highly attractive alternative—so much so that many a piece of furniture wears slipcovers all year. Certain furniture can even enjoy triple identity with an additional set of slipcovers.

The ideal time to arrange for slipcovers is at the purchase of the furniture. Interior designers will often coach their clients into having covers made when their custom sofa or chairs are in the workroom. More typically, the slipcover is an afterthought. It can be measured at home and made in a professional workshop. Or it can be homemade using easy sewing guidelines for fundamental styles. Even tossing a lightweight

fabric throw or large scarf over a chair constitutes a stylish covering.

Slipcovers, like clothing, go through changes in fashion. What is favored by most designers is the loose-fitting look, particularly on well-cushioned upholstered pieces. "Slipcovers should never imitate upholstery," says New York designer Richard Langham.

The traditional slipper chair (above) is a prime candidate for slipcovers. Because of its simple lines, covering can be accomplished with a minimum of tailoring. Stripes emphasize the graceful silhouettes and are precisely fitted to the chairs.

Chairs imitate tableware (left). The designs of German porcelain plates were painted on fabric by Georgia artist Susan Welsh for the home of interior designer, Dan Carithers. The front and back of the chair covers depict both sides of the plates.

The sheerest form of slipcover (opposite) was conceived by New York designers Simone Feldman and Victoria Hagan. White organza reveals rather than conceals the Hepplewhite-style chairs.

Variety at the table makes for an interesting meal (above). Three slipper chairs have tailored covers of linen and cotton. Snuggly fitted to the chairs, the details of the covers are what would be considered dressmaker style—kick pleats and self piping. The fabric, though light, has a good endurance record.

The seating ensemble in a foyer (right) was designed by Dan Carithers to be warm and welcoming. The coral color accomplishes both, as do the French side chairs made to look even more gracious with linen slipcovers.

120

The slipcover as
formal attire: Connecticut
designer Anne
Mullin Segerson acknowledged
the carving of twin
ribbon-back chairs in two
different but
complementary slipcovers. For
one, a bouncy
print (opposite above
right) is generously
embellished with golden coins
and fringe; on the
other, everyday muslin (above)
is dressed up with
ribbons of turquoise beads.

Sheets make an
overstuffed sofa (above right)
look ready for a
garden party. Leslie Allen used
one striped queen and
two floral queen flats to fashion
the cover.

New Orleans
designers Holden & Dupuy
amplify the lightness
of a living room (right) with
canvas slipcovers. As
easy fitting as covers can get
without looking
unkempt, they nonetheless
conform to the
shapes of the chairs and sofa.

versatile coffee tables

A circular tray table
(above) has an openwork base
that is also rounded,
echoing the curves of the sofa.
This shape coffee
table remedies the problem of
getting around sharp
corners. The scale of the table is
substantial, making it
within reach of people on both
sofa cushions. Its
dark surface sets off a collection
of cranberry glass.

Named for the beverage introduced in the early seventeenth century, the coffee table has become habit forming. For good reason. It's a necessary adjunct to the sofa and essential to the surrounding chairs.

Reputed to be the only piece of furniture invented in the twentieth century, the coffee table is perhaps the most versatile. It stands ready to hold cocktails, books, lamps, plants, pots, dessert, as well as coffee. While its name implies a specific purpose, the variations on the table are unlimited. Materials can range from alabaster to zebra wood, shapes from square to undulating. The coffee table can be one level, two levels, or a nest.

In some circumstances, an ottoman may serve as the coffee table, its height appropriate for outstretched legs. In fact, just about the only criterion for interpreting a coffee table is height. Level with the sofa seat is generally acceptable, or sixteen to twenty inches high, according to decorator Bill Hodgins. He views the coffee table as part of an ensemble and says, "I think people are more comfortable with two side tables and a coffee table." To that end he often places very low tables on either side of the sofa, with architectural floor lamps nearby.

As important looking as its role, this cherrywood table (right) is ample enough to work or dine on. Its Biedermeier style relates to the rest of the furnishings. The burled top has an extension drawer, convenient for serving hors d'oeuvres or holding flowers.

The living room of Colin Smith's California house (right) has the zest of New Mexican chilies, particularly in its coffee table. Artist Chuck Rowan created the individualistic piece with loglike legs and painted details that have a kinship with Indian blankets. Its long, pepper-colored surface, lacquered for glossy protection, is big enough for a buffet supper by the fire.

123

setting a dining table

That decorating credo—suitability—gains new clout when applied to the dining table. As one of the most serviceable pieces of furniture in a house, the table must fulfill certain requirements. For one, it has to comfortably accommodate a specific number of guests. A table's comfort level relates to its size and shape, which lead to the next requirement—hospitality, or the manner in which the scene is set.

The round table is renowned for being hospitable. It often solves the problem of fitting upwards of four people in a small area. "More intimate" is how Connecticut designer Anne Mullin Segerson sees round dining tables. Her personal choice for her 14-foot-square dining room is a round mahogany table that can comfortably accommodate six to eight. For Sunday brunches, Ms. Segerson uses informal round tablecloths and exposes the table and its inlaid starburst. For dinner occasions, the table's manner becomes more formal, with white linen placemats and many candles.

Ideally, a room is conceived with the table in mind. One such situation was an architect-designed house built according to small specifications, but following the notion

that the dining room should be a formal place to entertain. This concept yielded a 12-by-19-foot dining room whose table can comfortably hold up to a dozen people. Suitability, after all, depends on comfort.

The richness of a well-polished mahogany table (left) is played up by heirloom silver and white accessories. The centerpiece, mainly peonies and roses, is purposely low.

Making a placemat of fabric (below) matching the window borders was designer Freya Block's innovation for a Scandinavian-style dining room.

A dining table set for six (opposite) can accommodate twice as many. In a 12-by-19-foot room decorated by Robert K. Lewis, the rectangular table was chosen for its length and narrow width, a most efficient shape. The table is decorated in country fashion.

side tables: born to serve

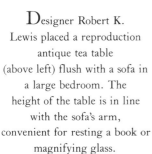

Designer Robert K. Lewis placed a reproduction antique tea table (above left) flush with a sofa in a large bedroom. The height of the table is in line with the sofa's arm, convenient for resting a book or magnifying glass.

A compact dining room (above center) can handle six at the round table, with a side table available for buffet service. Its marble top makes it durable enough to hold food platters and amenable to the display of sunflowers.

An antique tray table (above right) can be used for serving tea from a nearby chair. The height of a coffee table, it is easily moved as needed alongside or in front of a sofa.

Designer Anne Mullin Segerson's dining room (opposite) has similar tables on facing walls for regular use at mealtime or otherwise. Her Wedgewood tea service stands ready on a 17th-century country French table.

In a fashionable house of seventeenth-century Paris, dinner guests were catered to at a lavish banquet table. Nearby stood another, much smaller table, whose single purpose was to hold a ewer and basin with a towel for the after-dinner ritual of washing and drying the hands. The side table, born to serve, has been a vital member of the household for generations, wherever there was need for a place to put down a teacup, to set out a buffet, or to display flowers.

The side table is an indispensable piece of furniture, as necessary next to an armchair as it is near a dining table. Even when the side table is not being used as a serving or holding area, it plays an energetic role in the day-to-day life of a room. Versatile in its roles, the side table can be as peripatetic as its size allows.

Some styles, like those designed by John Saladino, are on casters so that the table that stands by a sofa on one occasion may be used elsewhere on another. The dining room usually hosts permanent side tables, or what have been traditionally known as sideboards, with drawers for utensils and linens. Abbreviated versions of the sideboard can be as basic as a period piece or a straight-legged rectangular table without drawers. Matching its multiple purposes are the side table's many guises—all of which aim to serve.

decorating in a vase

Ranunculus the color of citrus fruit (above left) are massed in an ironstone pitcher. The white container is a soothing contrast to the hot-colored flowers, which have a particularly strong impact en masse.

A riot of spring flowers (above center) makes a rounded composition with each shape distinct. Delphiniums are the tallest, their blue and purple spires intensifying the surrounding roses, tulips, and peonies. Queen Anne's lace provides contrast.

The country pitcher (above right) is a suitable choice for a primitive chest. Its contents, delphiniums and Queen Anne's lace, are arranged in a curve.

Composing an arrangement of flowers is decorating in a vase. The same principles of color, scale, and harmony apply as if the vase were a room. Editing what stays in and evaluating its shape is as vital a step as the flower selection.

The thoughtfully composed arrangement has individually beautiful flowers. And because each is unique, no two flowers will behave the same from day to day. Knowing the habits of certain flowers helps when making decisions about which will mingle best—similar to putting together a guest list. Apropos of suitable arrangements is the destination of the flowers. If they are to be at the dinner table, for example, the scale would have to be low enough not to obscure guests. Individual bud vases at each place setting are refreshing alternatives to the centerpiece—and solve the potential problem of flowers in guests' faces.

Nonchalance and spontaneity have become the prevailing styles in flower arrangements. The best rule of thumb: Follow the way the garden grows in drifts, with smaller forms graduating into larger varieties. Like the garden that looks unplanned, but actually has been years in the cultivating, successful flower arranging is well-thought-out.

The first reaction to a flower usually is to its color; the urge to sniff comes next. Studying the flower paintings of the Impressionists or visiting botanical gardens refines the color sense and develops individual preferences. Floral compositions can become signatures, with a hint of Manet, perhaps. "One has the illusion of being an artist painting a picture," said legendary English gardener Vita Sackville-West, "putting a dash of colour here, taking out another dash of colour there, until the whole composition is to one's liking." Her gardens illustrate on a large scale the effects of color that can be so beautifully and artfully condensed in a vase.

A confection of roses
(above), colored like Jordan
almonds, are tightly
bunched to conform with the
roundness of their
oriental bowl. If picked as
buds, roses will
develop to more than three
times their size. Steps
to increase the lifespan of roses
including picking
them early in the morning.

Hydrangeas (left)
were picked at varying stages of
maturity; their heads
naturally change shades from
white to assorted
pinks. Massed in a bucket on a
twig stand, they
become dried flowers without
water. They continue
to dry colorfully.

Cream-colored tulips repeat the tone of a dining room where they are the centerpiece. The largest pot of a trio of earthenware (above left) holds more than a dozen uncrowded tulips that contrast with the dark wood table.

Solid yellow and variegated tulips, early harbingers of spring (center left), are casually massed in a tin pot straight from the garden. Particularly hardy types, the tulips will color the room for days.

A group of dahlias run the spectrum from pale to brilliant (below left). The choice of pitcher was purposely a neutral color so as not to detract from the joviality of the flowers.

Shades of a cottage garden appear in a flowered room (far left). A crowd of ranunculus, viburnum, and tea roses make chubby bouquets in pitchers of similar roundness.

Peonies celebrate the arrival of spring with a burst of color and aroma (left). A few columbines present themselves like ballet dancers in the midst of their more voluptuous partners. The vase, with its base relief, provides a distinct contrast and interest in its own right.

Growing naturally, clumps of grass and all, these paperwhites (above) were cultivated from bulbs set on a layer of pebbles inside the wooden crate. Their fragrance can permeate a whole room.

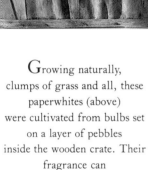

Bicolored tulips are surrounded with early spring whites (right), all long stemmed and in scale with their antique urns. The curve of the stems complements those of the containers. A white urn has the same lacy quality as its contents.

environmental design

In the beginning, there were tree trunks for tables and boulders for seats. Now, when choices include far more lavish furnishings, some people's creature comforts are still satisfied with tree trunks for tables and boulders for seats—or other permutations of the rustic and primitive.

One of the contemporary pioneers of organic designs was Michael Taylor, a Californian whose fresh-looking rooms inspired a rugged, yet refined genre of decorating. Another individualist, Ron Mann, respects the found object for its textural interest and unique blemishes. For over forty years, his northern California firm has been creating with the assistance of nature, a kind of scavenger-style design atelier. Mr. Mann is the penultimate beachcomber who ventures out after winter storms to look for driftwood that has been so washed it resembles bone. Subbasements of Bay Area houses provide him with unmilled lumber that he stockpiles and reworks: "I clean up mellow Douglas fir and sand it to get rid of the spurs and bad parts. Then I bleach it, sometimes twice."

The naturalist designer is a breed of environmentalist who sees beauty in imperfection, wonder in the stray object. On one of his many trips to Majorca, Mr. Mann discovered nearly extinct stone thrashers used for centuries to crush almonds and olives. The fluted stone ultimately became his signature lamp. Of that ingenuity, he says, "It's the old decorator's cliche. When you don't know what to do with something, make a lamp out of it."

The living room of designer Melanie Martin's California house (above) has rough-textured walls as a natural background for primitive woods, including random-shaped poles holding unhemmed canvas curtains.

Recessed shelves (opposite) hold a collection of abandoned bird's nests and primitive pottery—with no artificial color or preservatives added.

Consistent with the
rest of the house, the bedroom
is monochromatic,
with driftwood, stone, and
canvas its major
materials. The "cactus lamp," a
Ron Mann design,
stands nearly as tall as the
improvised
headboard, actually an old
screen. All the
recycled wood was assembled
with pegs and bolts;
no chemical glues were used.

quality of light

An adobe-style
house in California (above and
opposite) was
designed with consideration for
the quality of light.
Its most vital source is the
outdoors—a hillside
and vineyard—to which the
house responds with
multiple windows of all sizes,
from small squares
to walls of glass. Colors and
textures were used
to amplify the naturally light
house. Owner and
interior designer Toby Flax
incorporated ambient
as well as task light in the form
of overhead spots, a
chandelier over the dining
table, and a floor
lamp stationed by the sofa.

"In all the equipment of the modern house," said Elsie de Wolfe circa 1913, "there is nothing more difficult than the problem of artificial light. To have the right light properly distributed so that the rooms may be suffused with just the proper glow, but never a glare; so that the base outlets for reading-lamps shall be at convenient angles, so that the wall lights shall be beautifully balanced—all this means prodigious thought and care before the actual placing of the light is accomplished." While lighting styles may have changed dramatically over the decades, the challenges seem to remain the same.

A more recent evaluation comes from John Saladino who defines three spheres of lighting: ambience, work, and art. Ambience refers to the general illumination of the interior, its shapes and dimensions. The quality of light is important, but not the source, according to Saladino's view: "Lighting should never confront you; it should be hidden and beautifully orchestrated. The first task in designing a lighting plan is to conceal the source of light." This translates into recessed ceiling lights or those concealed in coves or behind the moldings.

With work light, the decision has to do with lamps. Saladino opts for an almost invisible variety—simple glass cylinders with silver transparent cord and white or ivory translucent shades because of the soft light they cast. The choice of bulb also contributes to the decision: the higher the wattage, the harsher the light. To illuminate art, built-in ceiling lights or a frame-mounted light from above should bathe paintings. Light can also be directed from the floor via can lights concealed in corners or behind plants and sculpture.

Saladino also talks in terms of spheres and zones, the latter relating to areas above the head, at eye level, and below the knees. The ideal situation would hit all three, with candlelight qualifying as a source of over-the-head or eye-level light. The optimum, of course, is natural light for almost every situation, be it a makeup table by a window, a bathroom with a skylight, or a dining room with a wall of glass.

Fitor a bedroom
whose style is of the English-
garden variety,
the reading lamps should
correspond. Here the
prerequisite bedside lamp suits
its environment
(right). The shade is gathered
and frilled, somewhat
like a skirt; the base is china
with florals in colors
related to the wallpaper
and linens.

Candlestick lamps
were fashioned into sconces
(right) that softly
light the fireplace area of a
child's room. Deep
green shades subdue the light,
which washes the
wall. The combination of brass
and green is repeated
in candlesticks on the mantel.

A track provides a
source of multiple and adjustable
overhead lights.
While this track (below) is white
to blend in with the
ceiling, the dome lights are
brass, related to the
other metals in the living room.

adorning the hearth

An elongated fireplace (above) is part of the "good bones" of an early 1900s house. A distinguishing feature in the bedroom, the fireplace has molding that adds dimension, with a black slate hearth and surround that frame dried flowers.

The room with a fireplace is privileged. It has a natural gathering place, a source of warmth, and more than likely a prominent wall on which to display artwork or hang a mirror. Fireplaces with architectural distinction like period molding or stonework elevate a room beyond the ordinary and give a head start to the decorating plan. The question of where to place a sofa and chairs is answered in the vicinity of the fireplace. If the bedroom happens to have one, the main vantage point would preferably be from the bed. As for the kitchen with a fireplace, this evokes desires for early morning loaves of bread straight from the hearth.

Since the 1600s, when French pattern books displayed important elements of interior architecture, the fireplace has been highly regarded for its ornamental value. Many engravings were devoted to the chimneypiece, which was the room's dominant feature. That early focal point has sustained its importance over the years, though becoming smaller in proportion. The opening was decreased thanks to Count Rumford's eighteenth-century changes, thereby reducing a fireplace's tendency to smoke. Also reduced was the amount of elaborate ornamentation above the fireplace. Mirrors, paintings, or sculptured relief became the fashion.

In fact, decorating a fireplace wall has endless interpretations. The popular choice of hanging a mirror —considered a cliché by some decorators—has as much to do with personal style as it does with the size of the room. If the space needs increasing, a mirror is the obvious solution. Hanging a painting, an ancestral or even animal portrait are other choices. A fireplace with a wall of flagstone is the setting for Indian artifacts; another of brick displays a carving from an old Sicilian apple cart. Carte blanche is in order when dressing a fireplace wall.

The fireplace reflects
the California living room of
designer Stephen
Shubel (above). By covering the
surround with
mirror, he captured light
coming in from the
opposite wall of windows. On
the mantel, a chair
drawn by a 19th-century French
decorator and a Balinese
mask indicate worldly taste.

In a large-scale
bedroom (right) designer
Robert K. Lewis
placed enormous urn-shaped
finials on a mantel
whose proportions were also
strong. The all-white
setting includes a collection of
lacy china, backed by
a plaster panel leaning against
the wall. A black
marble surround dramatizes
the effect.

White masonry (left) and a pale wood mantel make a clean background for the display of folk art. A functional part of the room, this is also a kind of gallery where even the andirons command attention.

Handcrafts are the theme of this fireplace (below) centered on a tongue-and-groove wall. The separate mantel, actually a shelf of wood molding, sits well above, leaving room for a pair of tin ornaments. A painted checkerboard forms the surround.

Designer Beverly Ellsley's Connecticut fireplace invites closer investigation (opposite). From the matching andirons to the rugged stones and inscribed mantel, the fireplace is an historical landmark for the house.

decorative screens

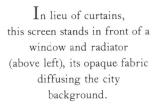

In lieu of curtains, this screen stands in front of a window and radiator (above left), its opaque fabric diffusing the city background.

The screen is a dominant architectural element (above center). Made of burled wood with arches, it serves as both a divider and a point of interest in an otherwise plain room.

Intricate needlepoint forms a three-panel screen (above right). Placed near a window and lamp, the screen enjoys both kinds of lighting to intensify its rich colors.

An antique French screen (opposite) has panels of wallpaper and a rustic wood frame that recalls country houses, where drafts were thwarted by the likes of this.

The screen is a decorating wizard—a practical tool or an art object. When Clark Gable hung a blanket to separate his bed from Claudette Colbert's in "It Happened One Night," he was designing a screen, albeit a crude one. Since the screen evolved from a piece of cloth, it has since been carved, etched, draped, and papered for a multitude of purposes, not the least of which is privacy. In fact, privacy has long been the screen's principal function—a provocative wall that allows for undressing or quick changes for the next scene. But the screen's role extends to all corners of the house, given its ability to alter the dimensions of a room, conceal an awkward space, cut off drafts, or simply stand there, an object of admiration.

Ornamental screens punctuate a room. They can take the form of a basic, three-fold design with wood slats (similar to louvered doors) painted a vivid color and strategically placed to fill a void. Such a screen is

an architectural device like a pillar that provides verticality and a sense of boundary. Another type of decorative screen is the picturesque, a painted mural that depicts a landscape, which can be moved to suit the needs of the room.

Some screens qualify as fine art and can become the starting point of decorating. For example, a lacquered oriental screen of several panels will establish a color scheme. Screens with a pedigree, such as a coromandel, often become a wall hanging or the room's main art object.

Apart from the practical and ornamental, some screens are designed to fill a particular purpose. One example is the mirrored screen—upwards of three panels that, when positioned in a certain way, add depth to an area. Another type of purposeful screen is one that divides space. Fretwork or lattice are good choices in those instances where the barest division is preferred.

144

One end of a bedroom (right) was furnished as if it were autonomous. The area is self-contained with plush seating slipcovered in white canvas and toile. The same pattern was used to upholster a four-paneled screen that fills a corner left exposed when the sofa was turned on an angle.

A curved screen that's based on the style of a Palladian window (below) appears to be looking out on the landscape of Tuscany. Painted by artist Trudy Solin, the three-fold screen and its decorative molding add to the architectural energy of a sunroom. Slim French doors, classical in style, are in themselves like screens.

A tall, three-paneled screen (opposite) fills one empty corner of a living room. Purchased as unfinished wood, the screen was spray painted yellow to give the room a spot of sunshine. The screen's height makes the vaulted ceiling less distant, thereby giving the room a more intimate scale.

147

the art of display

Decorating is as much about editing and arranging as it is about introducing new elements to a room. The skillful arranger can size up a room, take a vase from here, a bowl from there, and head for a tabletop. The vase and bowl then have different positions from which to be appreciated. The bowl may be filled with polished stones, the vase with ornamental grass. The result is a composition.

"The way people accumulate and display objects can add immeasurably to a room's vitality," said Billy Baldwin. He would encourage his celebrated clients to leave collections out in the open "as the English keep them—on tables and commodes where you can see them and touch them."

Not surprisingly, out in the open has become the preferred style of display. Objects are accessible for entertaining and add colorful ele-

Carpenter-made units (left) comprise a wall designed by Peter Wheeler to "organize chaos." With 12 inches of space per unit, his collection of white dinnerware gets separate but equal exposure. The unit is painted oil-based white for durability.

ments to the room as well. More kitchens have tableware exposed on shelves or visible through glass doors; porcelains and glass in dining rooms are displayed on side tables; fireplace mantels and even floors are exhibition areas in living rooms. Bathrooms, too, are likely to be display areas for collections of perfume bottles or antique mirrors.

The manner of organizing is determined by the decorating style. Baldwin's reference to English rooms evokes libraries and parlors brimming with old porcelains, animal portraits, and silver-framed pictures. For those whose taste runs to the more organized rather than the spontaneous, display would be an architectural element, such as a series of gridwork wall units. Designer Peter Wheeler created order for the library and dining area of his Boston townhouse by building symmetrical cases he claims are the new-generation orange crate—or sophisticated versions of the cubby hole. The 12-inch squares encourage organization, with the benefits being easy access and total visibility. There is aesthetic value, too, in that the all-white recessed unit presents handsomely, introducing a checkerboard pattern that's more energetic than plain horizontal shelves.

The mantel of a
faux-painted fireplace (right)
displays all things
black and white. The classical
theme is announced
by a Piranesi print of St. Peter's
in Rome. Two West
African urns, set on black
columns, stand like
sentries beside a collection of
salt-glazed teapots
with pewter lids. A tureen with
sphinx handles marks
the center.

A contemporary
version of the Windsor bench
(below) makes a
miniature art gallery of a
hallway. Animal
photographs are in line with the
spindled back and at
eye level for those seated.

The all-white
arrangement (top) includes a
plaster panel as
backdrop. A starfish is not out
of place with
heirloom china.

A weathered country
table (above) holds pottery of
similar character. The
framed print appears to be
another texture and is
actually an antique garden plan.

Pale walls and
bleached floors allow attention
to go directly to an
18th-century Shaker rocker and
earthenware pottery
(left). The shelves and pots
seem to be arranged
for each other, patterned
separate from plain.

151

Color energizes the
assortment of jovial pots (right)
that are displayed on a
primitive French Canadian
chest. Its red paint is
in harmony with the collection
as well as the pairs,
live and painted. Resting the
painting on the chest
agrees with the informality of
the situation.

The back of a sofa
could be treated as negative
space, but there is the
potential for using it as a display
area (above). Here, a
table nearly the same level as the
sofa shows off an
antique map and pottery.

A linear
arrangement of objects (right)
contributes to the
calm of this room. The shelves
hold books in
horizontal and vertical
formation with the
top shelf devoted to pottery of a
similar neutral color.

Real flowers (opposite)
seem to be an outgrowth of those
on the French antique
wallpaper. The floral theme is a
recurring one, from
the vases to a brass candleholder.

A collection of
ironstone china (above) is
coupled with wire
miniatures, its scale
emphasizing the doll-
sized furniture.

The living room
bears evidence of eclectic taste
(left). An iron
weather vane is silhouetted
against a white wall
pointing to another artifact of
Americana on the
piano. The coffee table also
holds a form of folk
art. The floor, too, is used for
display. Antique farm
containers are under the piano,
a wire birdcage on a
trunk next to the sofa.

155

functional storage

Every design solution begins with a question. Where storage is concerned, the quandries multiply, to the degree that a checklist would be in order. In fact, order is the essence of storage. And each room has particular demands, whether it be dining-room tableware, library books, or children's playthings.

Basically, there are two types of storage. One is open, the other closed. The open variety shows all, so the contents become decorative elements in the room. Certain pieces of furniture—the hutch or break-front—fall into the open category.

Then there are the wall shelves and cubby holes—carpenter details

built into the room's architecture so they appear to have always been there. Closed storage can range from an armoire to an antique trunk. A contemporary invention by an architect could take the form of a free-standing wall or a room divider.

The choice of freestanding, built-in, or modular styles (systems that can be added to) depends on the suitability to the room. A shelf unit built to match the architectural details of a paneled library would serve it well. Modular units, from plastic stacking bins to labeled cardboard boxes, suit the ever-changing needs of children's rooms or the utilitarian requirements of home offices.

Designer Peter Wheeler improvised dining room storage (above) with store-bought bookshelves. Because the cases are hung at the same level as the dining table, they can also function as a side table. Space underneath can be used for storing baskets.

"We have a book problem," says Nancy Goslee Power, whose library fills a specially built wall unit (opposite); on top are white speakers. The unit's molding matches that of the living room's fireplace.

156

A thoughtfully
planned child's room (right) has
just about everything
built in which encourages
putting everything in
its place. An 8-by-10-foot loft
hung from two beams
makes a duplex of the room
with cubby holes as
part of the stair unit. The
9-foot-high room has
every inch accounted for,
storage being the
major element. The bunk bed,
too, has storage as
part of its design. Rather
than a conventional
headboard, there are units for
storing bedtime
books.

The nook of a
cottage bedroom (right) has
been turned into a
miniature gallery for folk art
and assorted crafts.
The built-in storage unit is
basic: horizontal
wood shelves with vertical
dividers. The top
shelf allows for display while
the bottom unit
houses books and pictures. A
small chair, one of the
owners' many Southwestern
pieces, works as a
portable book shelf.

Because lockers
inspire organization, this child's
room (above) takes
the idea as its theme. Each of
the vertical "lockers"
has storage space for hanging
clothes; the lower bins
house other gear. Using storage
walls in this way
elminates the need for much
freestanding
furniture. Here one chest is the
only other furnishing
necessary apart from the bed.

Walls of a child's
room (above right) have been
designed for serious
use with a playful attitude. The
two-level bleachers
are roomy in themselves and
lift up into storage
bins. They've been made more
realistic with trompe
l'oeil painting—grass, nails,
butterflies, and all.

The corner of an
apartment (right) was deemed
appropriate for a
library. Using the window as a
ledge, the owner
designed a system based on
cubby holes, each one
uniform and as large as the
biggest book. With a
selected number of books to
each compartment,
titles are quickly spotted, books
easily removed.

159

An antique gilt chest (right) fills the corner of a living room that has minimal shelves. Therefore, this has been designated a miniature library, with a classical bust stationed on the ground level.

One wall of a dining room (below) was crafted into a cupboard with custom-made wood cabinetry and finished off with crown molding to make it a cohesive part of the room. Its window ledge serves as a buffet while the cabinets store all tableware and linens.

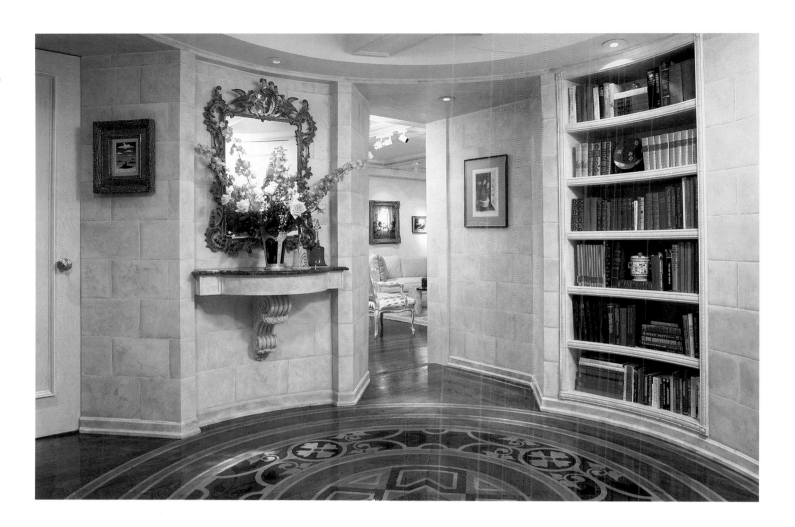

In the small foyer of
a fifties apartment designers
Lynn Jacobson and
Richard Orbach responded to
the owners' need
for storage (this page).
A central
hall with doors leading to the
kitchen, bedroom,
and living room was given new
dignity as well as
purpose with the invention of a
circular space that
houses a closet concealed by
bookshelves. One
compartment fits into another
and can be opened
with a touch. Ceiling spots
illuminate both the
bookshelves and the closet. The
floor, marquetry
created with paint, expands on
the circular theme.

161

kitchen storage

Glass-fronted cabinets (left) allow for the display of attractive pottery, while other items are behind a solid door. Cabinets flank the dishwasher.

Nearly every pot and important utensil in the house hangs over the cooktop (below). This is open storage at its most accessible. Visible, too, are spices arranged in a glass-fronted cabinet.

A kitchen's success is the result of planning and prior experience. Storage and work space are vital elements in the master plan. The kitchen is as dependent on them as a recipe is on the proper amount of needed ingredients.

One principle, based on observations of kitchen remodelers, is that for every work area there should be storage space. The work island, for example, needs cabinets for pots and drawers for utensils. If the island is also an eating station, storage is needed for tableware and linens. The range and refrigerator also require storage space outside of themselves—cupboards for cookware and shelves for baking tools, unopened bottles, canned foods, and nonperishable ingredients.

The sink zone demands closed storage space for cleaning equipment and garbage units. If there is a kitchen table, it should have built-in drawers or a nearby cupboard to hold daily necessities. A kitchen pantry is the ultimate storage unit. A timeless idea that has evolved from the most hospitable old kitchens, the pantry's cupboard with glass doors is ideal.

The pantry is an independent unit (opposite) with its own lighting system and shelves that hold all the family china and copper, plus canned and bottled goods. Strategically placed on a major wall of the kitchen, the cupboard is near the wall ovens and work counter where its contents are regularly used.

The horizontal space
of this kitchen (left) would limit
its efficiency if it
weren't for a well-thought-out
storage wall. Upper
and lower cabinets fulfill all the
daily needs for dishes
and cookware. Tall end cabinets
function as
cupboards. Open shelves relieve
the density of solid
cabinets and hold some of the
more decorative
pieces. The room's width is
visually increased by
the mirrored backsplash; and
the absence of
hardware on the cabinets also
helps to open the
room.

A traditional kitchen
(left) is divided by a work
island that provides
ample storage for cooking
equipment and daily
linens. Molding on the
cabinetry is in
keeping with the room's
architecture. Cabinets
above the counter have panes
similar to the
windows; their contents are no
secret.

Organization is vital
to the cook. Here is optimum
efficiency (this page).
An obscure area underneath a
seating unit was made
into storage compartments for
infrequently used platters.
The banquette seats two guests
above the storage. The
work zone of the kitchen has as
much variety of storage as
a chef has knives.

kitchen countertops

The kitchen without efficient countertops is like a laundry room without an ironing board. Work can be done, but with difficulty. Counters serve the chef as an assistant would, being available to hold pots, organize ingredients, and roll out the dough. The ideal kitchen anticipates every situation and responds with versatility.

The variety of materials available for countertops is a matter of multiple choice, depending upon the tasks, budget, and desired aesthetics. Counters have evolved into a kind of furniture, some of hardwood, others of stone or tile, and still more of synthetic materials that are sometimes both resilient and colorful.

Once the kitchen counter used to be reserved for hard work in utilitarian rooms where doors were closed during cooking and guests never ventured. With the advent of country kitchens, where the activity of cooking became communal and often as not meals were taken, the counter came to act as a dining table.

The island and the peninsula were developed as the purpose of kitchens was multiplied—from work spaces to eating areas to gathering places. These independent elements allow for variation in the way space is used. A center island, for example, turns that area into a work station, leaving the periphery for storage and more counter surface. If the island contains a cooktop, the choice of counter must take into account the material's heat resistancy. And since chopping usually takes place near the cooktop, a wooden butcher block would also increase efficiency. The peninsula, too, serves a variety of purposes. In fact, the most well-equipped kitchen will have more than one type of counter surface—the ingredient that makes the most efficient kitchens.

An apartment kitchen (above), open to the living room, has one counter that doubles as an eating area. Resilient, highly polished marble counters make fine furniture out of the cabinets.

The counter that is also a room divider (above left) has a stepped-up partition and a marble surface at a height comfortable for standing and serving.

Counters reserved for hard work (opposite) are butcher block on either side of the range. The double-duty island is covered with sturdy large tiles. When not being used for dining, the surface is a washing and chopping center.

White laminate
countertops under the cabinets
and on the island
support the pristine quality of
this kitchen
(opposite). On both sides of the
cooktop are protective
boards for collecting hot food.
The main kitchen
sink has a tile surface for
plant care.

Tile covers all the
counters in a kitchen based on a
blue-and-white color
scheme (above). The tile pattern
is reminiscent of
kitchen towels with its fresh-
looking gridwork. It
also complements a pottery
collection.

The sum of this
weekend-house kitchen (above
right) is its
counters—thick slabs of
limestone with highly
polished surfaces and rugged
edges. Custom-made
by a tile and marble company,
the countertops
suggest the coastline just
outside.

A built-in cupboard
(right) includes a wood buffet
counter for serving
the dining table.

169

dressing the bed

The expression "hitting the hay" used to be a literal description of going to bed. That was prior to the eleventh century when a bed was just a humble sack of straw laid on the floor. A few centuries later, beds became significant pieces of furniture, one of the more notable being England's Great Bed of Ware made during the 1500s and measuring about 11-feet-square—large enough to accommodate four couples side by side. Subsequently, beds evolved into more intimate quarters, shrinking in proportion to rooms that were no longer reception halls, but sleeping chambers for one or two. That modern-day beds range from futons on the floor to draped and canopied four-posters suggests styles have come full circle. Even the water bed, considered a modern invention, had a predecessor. In the nineteenth century, the water-filled mattress became therapy for hospitalized patients.

No piece of furniture is as essential to one's well-being as the bed. Its significance prompted Guy de Maupassant to write: "The bed, my friend, is our whole life. It is there that we are born, it is there that we love, it is there that we die. . . ." That is a huge amount of responsibility for one piece of furniture, but then again the bed is where most of us spend one-third of our lives. How it feels accounts for its importance.

Making a decision about the type of bed to be purchased involves a major investment of time and money. Considerations include the suitability of size and firmness of the mattress—in other words, the essen-

The all-upholstered bed (left) has dual personality curtains, the exposed pattern being an oriental print. The lining is a graphic arrangement of stripes. The pillow cases and top sheet are reminiscent of quilt designs, with the burgundy, cream, and deep green synthesizing the room's colors.

A black iron four-poster (below) is dressed in the manner of windows, with curtains tied to the rods and hung to the floor. Sprays of flowers on the curtain seem to be miniature versions of those on the bedcover.

tials of comfort. As with a sofa, the better the initial investment, the longer the bed's life span.

Bed dressing, too, has centuries of style. The luxury of down-stuffed pillows goes back to ancient Rome; piling many pillows on the bed is associated with the Middle East. The curtained and canopied bed recalls the English four-poster; the futon, Japan; the duvet, France; the eiderdown comforter, Germany. How a bed is dressed relates to the design of a room, be it romantic or Shaker simplicity. If the result is comfort, the bed has been successfully addressed.

A carved,
four-poster bed (left) was
tailored for a room
that also contains a sitting area.
Bachelor chests act as
end tables, with ample storage
for clothing or linens.
Designed by Nelson Ferlita, the
room gets its color
energy from an antique quilt
and peach walls,
whose molding has been painted
white for contrast.

In this bedroom
designed by Keith Irvine (below)
he set what he terms
"a very good Chippendale bed
at a whimsical angle
to quietly mix up and warm the
room." Evocative of
warmth is the deep blue lining
of the canopy.

A bed and reading
nook all in one (above) is the
brainchild of
California designer
Gep Durenberger.
His Mediterranean-style house
has antiques and
books galore, many of which
reside in the bedroom.

Price was an object
in a bedroom decorated by
New York's Georgina
Fairholme (above right). The
major investment went
toward the chintz fabric that
upholsters the bed
from headboard to dust ruffle.
Another valuable
ingredient is the antique quilt
whose colors
synthesize the room's palette.

The idea of a sofa
inspired this bed (right),
upholstered legs and
all. Unlike most beds, this gets
unmade in the
morning. Mattress and box
spring are always
presentable, covered in a print
that makes the room
feel like a garden.

The rustic beams of
a cottage (above) are of the same
character as the
antique iron beds. A guest
room, as this is,
appears more gracious when
furnished with twin
beds for a weekend in the
country. Tattersall
blankets and chrocheted cases,
along with homespun
checks, are joined by ruffled,
floral sheets—bed
dressing at its most creative.

Somewhat like a
window seat (above), this sleigh
bed is tucked into an
alcove. Its coziness is ensured
with a stack of plump
pillows allowing the guest a
closer view out the
window. Two necessary
accessories, a reading
lamp and table, are at bedside.

Decorating can be
pared down to a minimum of
objects sensitively
combined (above right). This
room has the air of a
country inn, with its white pine
sleigh bed and
stylized flower quilt.

The smallest of
bedrooms (left) could be a cabin
in the woods. It is
both guestroom and a collector's
respository for
Western paraphernalia. The
wagon-wheel bed is
situated between two windows
for cross ventilation.
A coverlet of striped cotton
matches the cushions
of the wicker rocking chair. An
antique pillow case
has a new ruffle, the colors of
which are picked up
in the Hopalong Cassidy wall
border.

Respect for the pine
trees native to northern Georgia
inspired these
handmade twin beds (left).
In fact, homeowner
Comer Jennings took every
opportunity to
incorporate rustic materials into
his lakeside cottage.
Yet, the only color in this tiny
guest bedroom comes
from afar—the appliqué
coverlets were made
in Thailand.

This nautical room
(above) was designed by
Jeannette Renauley
for a young boy in Alabama.
Sails were cut from
plywood, then padded and
covered in striped
cotton. Welting was added to
the dust ruffles to
reinforce their shape. Angled
valances resemble
awnings and the striped welting
cord suggests molding.

intimate dressing tables

The bedroom of an early 19th-century house (right) contains the owner's collection of Victorian dressing table objects and the flavor of Sweden in its heirloom lace.

A country dressing table (opposite) was improvised with a one-drawer pine table and an embroidered linen towel. The painted pine mirror, tall enough to hang inside a closet door, leans against the wall. Antique glass and silver accessories were collected over the years.

Throughout history, the dressing table has been an indispensable aid in a woman's daily beauty ritual. The furnishing's importance to a woman is equaled by its impact on the decoration of a room. The style of the table tells much about the woman in the mirror.

There is a seventeenth-century engraving that depicts an English lady's bedchamber, most likely in a house designed by the great architect Indigo Jones. The most striking aspect of the room is its dressing table covered with a fringed carpet and another layer of linen trimmed in lace (called a toilette).

Another engraving of similar vintage shows a Danish bedchamber with a woman standing at her dressing table, which is covered with a fringed cloth. She is looking into a small mirror that stands on top of the table. Next to the mirror sits a warming device for the curling iron she holds. With it, she is creating side curls, the rage of the day. Yet another early picture reveals a Dutch woman's dressing table, covered with a table carpet. It holds cases for her toiletries.

Flashing forward to modern day, we find dressing tables in all sorts of garb. There are the ultra-feminine varieties wearing lace petticoats with ruffled skirts. More tailored types have piping instead of ruffles and perhaps a striped skirt. When the top of a table is covered with fabric, it is desirable to protect it with glass or mirror. In the case of an antique, a drawer or tray may hold the assorted toiletries. Yet, not all dressing tables need decoration. A lacquered table from the twenties, for example, deserves being seen.

No dressing table can exist without a mirror, either one that is attached or one that stands like a picture frame. As has been the case throughout the ages, a hand mirror is another essential tool for closeups in a lady's private space.

Sheets dress a long,
narrow table in the style of a
gown (above).
The three-tiered arrangement
has an underskirt
overlaid with puckered scallops
and a border of red.
A slab of glass covers the top.

A Scandinavian-style
bedroom has its dressing table
topped with a ribbon-
framed mirror (above right).
Sidelights are antique
brass lamps with frosted globes
for ultra-soft
illumination. The table, covered
in floral cotton, wears
a lace flounce.

Bed coverings
provide the fabric for a double-
skirted dressing table
(right). Its underskirt is
gathered and
interlined, forming a luxurious
drape. A lacy blanket
cover is pinned up like a bustle.

A collector's dressing
table (this page) harks back to
earlier centuries with
its accoutrements of beauty.
What isn't ivorine is
old silver. Assorted frames hold
nostalgic pictures,
and a silver-topped bottle
contains dusting
powder. Conical vases hold
delicate bouquets
of cyclamen and lilies-of-the-
valley, while
a footed bowl adds the aroma of
potpourri. The table
itself is dressed with a flounced
pattern similar
to the pleated lamp shades.

personalizing
the bath

In the history of dwellings, the bathroom is young. Not until the nineteenth century was the bathroom integrated into the design of a home. It was rural architect Andrew Jackson Downing whose house plans placed a water closet in the same room with the tub. Consequently, turn-of-the-century American bathrooms were built just large enough to house three utilitarian fixtures.

The bathroom has since made up for lost time as a respected section of the house. It has become perhaps the most pampered room, coinciding with the value placed on fitness and well-being. The care lavished on a bathroom has become symbolic of self-esteem. Moreover, the room that was once sequestered with no relevance to the rest of the decor is now often an adjunct to the bedroom or, at the very least, an inviting aspect of the home.

Evelyn Waugh in *Brideshead Revisited* recorded his memories of a particular bathroom with a "deep, copper, mahogany-framed bath, that was filled by pulling a brass lever heavy as a piece of marine engineering." He went on to describe "the huge towel warming on the back of the chintz armchair" in contrast to the "clinical little chambers glittering with chromium-plate and looking-glass which pass for luxury in the modern world."

Modern standards of luxury run the gamut from handcrafted woods and greenhouse windows to state-of-the-art whirlpool baths with spalike amenities, including soaking tubs and exercise equipment. If price is no object, the bath can be the most

self-indulgent of rooms, with multi-jet showers and wall-to-wall marble.

For the house proud of its history, the bathroom can be fitted with period details, from a pedestal sink to antique-looking hardware and mosaic tile floors. And for the house with antique-quality fixtures, decoration may be a simple matter of cosmetics, say, a new wallpaper or shower curtain.

The accessories of the bath contribute to its efficiency as well as to its aesthetics. They also make the difference between a clinical environment and a creative one. Country house bathrooms invite the most improvisation, with old baskets as hampers, flea-market mirrors in lieu of medicine chests, and framed samplers as artwork. That the bathroom is the youngest part of the house does not mean it must look the most modern, only the most comfortable.

The master bath of a small, custom-built house is based on a grid, with black-and-white tiles and glass brick adhering to the format (opposite). Large tiles form a border on the mirror and tub, with smaller tiles as the floor design. The largely mirrored wall doubles the room's pattern while adding its reflective quality.

A stencil need not be confined to walls (above left). Here it's applied to an Edwardian cast-iron tub, transforming it from an outdated relic to functional art. English artist Lyn Le Grice applied her craft with stencils she designed. The tub's wavelike pattern is colored to relate to the walls, which have a stenciled paisley border.

The confined space of a cottage bathroom (above) is thoroughly decorated, from stenciled borders around the arched window to delft tiles set into terra-cotta squares. A vintage porcelain sink, appealing on its own, is made more noticeable by the double skirt it wears.

CHAPTER FOUR

GREAT TRANSFORMATIONS

decorating success stories

Achieving harmony, color, and scale throughout an entire house is the ultimate accomplishment. Combining the various elements may mean working in stages, over a period of months or even years, with a vision in mind. That vision can be inspired by a personal passion, by a particular region or landscape, or by the house itself. Though financial dictates may prevail, demanding that work be completed in stages, once the vision is established, the rest eventually falls into place.

Often a house is itself unique; it may have been a church, or a school, or a gristmill. In such a case, the owner knowingly takes on a responsibility to the original structure, to preserve its identity while imbuing it with residential comfort. In a Greek Revival schoolhouse, for instance, new owners refused to tamper with the architectural lines of the building. Their addition extends from the rear, so that the school appears from the street as it did one hundred years ago. In another instance, a gristmill was adopted by two people with intentions to preserve its eccentricities. A dramatic structure to begin with, considering its stone facade and dark-wood beamed ceilings, it became a highly theatrical home.

Some of the most successful homes reflect the avid interests of their owners. After all, home is the most appropriate setting for celebrations of passionate pursuits. One featured here is the domain of a Francophile whose decorating style is two-parts Provençal, one part improvisational. In another, an American-ideal house of white clapboard and brick, the owners recycled parts of the original house in an ambitious remodeling project so that everything fused.

Such design considerations might be envied by those who are the first residents in a house. With its flawless white walls and spotless woodwork, a new house may seem terribly sterile and clinical. The greatest advantage is being able to collaborate with the architect beforehand. The small house shown here exemplifies the successful collaboration of architect and designer, who both infused it with expansive ideas. Because of the level of comfort in every room, this new house is destined to age gracefully.

Different as they are, diverse as their owners, these homes have comfort in common. It's what the grand master Billy Baldwin described as "knowing that if someone pulls up a chair for a talk, the whole room doesn't fall apart." The editors of *House Beautiful* have selected each of the houses because it successfully transcends its components to become a harmonious whole. Each epitomizes a great transformation.

a renovated schoolhouse

The dream of living in the country is usually associated with visions of historic houses and rooms with furniture of sentimental value. Neither vision nor sentiment was in short supply for Murray and Albert Douglas when they purchased an abandoned 1890 Greek Revival schoolhouse in upstate New York for weekends away from their city work. A watercolor rendered by Mrs. Douglas attested to their vision, with a good deal of sentiment as well. Whereas the painting was meant to convince country bankers of the sincerity of their renovation, it also succeeded in making the new owners' dreams feasible. To preserve the identity of the old schoolhouse and make it habitable, the Douglases divided the structure into a living room and kitchen on the first floor, with bedrooms located on the second and attic stories. Once the structural changes were accomplished, the next challenge was decorating with respect for their inherited antiques. To that end Mrs. Douglas engaged the help of Connecticut designer Nan Heminway. A decorating style evolved that put emphasis on timelessness and comfort.

The schoolhouse's 12-foot-high walls were painted the

The 1890 schoolhouse (above) was rendered in watercolor by owner Murray Douglas to show exterior improvements.

The living room (right) measures 21 by 36 feet, an ample enough room to handle dark Victorian antiques and vivid fabric patterns.

The fireplace in the
dining room (left) has
a symmetrical
arrangement on the mantel.

color of cream with semi-gloss white woodwork, a contrast typical of the Greek Revival period. The choice of background color was influenced also by the nature of the furnishings, most of which were dark wood. The lightness and volume of space seemed to invite pattern, or even several. Mrs. Douglas opted for one and lots of it. As an executive in Brunschwig & Fils, a fabric house renowned for its documented patterns, she had no problem finding material. Her problem was making a choice. She eventually gravitated to a cotton print called Borromea for the sofa and chairs. Its exuberance fills the two-story space with hefty amounts of red, an appropriate color to balance the Victorian antiques inherited from her husband's family.

Ten years of living in the schoolhouse (purchased in 1968 for $5,000) whetted the owners' appetites for more comfortable rooms to accommodate guests. The next project in the growth of the schoolhouse was a substantial addition that actually tripled the building's size and, in

Hinting of
Scandanavia, the dining room
(below) features a painted
chest and slipcovered chairs.

The former master bedroom (opposite) is located in the original schoolhouse. Its bed has a partial canopy with trapping. The new master bedroom (below) has a full-fledged canopy and a headboard upholstered to match the lining and wallpaper.

doing so, reinforced its historic identity. The two structures interrelate, yet are independent of one another. The addition has heat while the schoolhouse does not; therefore, come winter, the modernized rooms substitute for the antique. Because the newer wing has no living room, its dining room serves that function as well as its own. Guests can gather around the fireplace as they would in a traditional living room or sit by the large Palladian window, a source of solar warmth. The room's peach tone is as complementary as natural sunshine. While the walls appear to be decoratively painted, they are actually covered in wallpaper, a more affordable alternative.

Decorating the newer wing required an acknowledgment of the older structure so that the two became cohesive. Details are true to the Greek Revival fluted window and doorframes and paneled wood doors. Painted furniture also contributes to the dining room's neoclassical flavor.

The master bedroom was positioned near the dining room to make the addition somewhat like a private apartment. Indeed, the bedroom is a sanctuary with its compact

space dominated by an "always wanted" canopy bed facing a fireplace. Draped, skirted, and fringed, the sleeping quarter harks back to eighteenth-century bed furniture, a style in which many different fabric treatments are combined in one outfit. Approximately 35 yards of patterned fabric were used to dress the queen-sized bed, including the dust ruffle. The lining, repeated in the wallpaper, took another 40 yards. A border around the room is fabric tape in colors that relate to the bed. With all the enveloping fabric, the bed is like a room unto itself, lit by two swing-arm lamps. Slits were cut into the shirred trapping so the lamps would be integrated. Underneath all the bed hangings is a framework attached to the ceiling to form the square. The valance, therefore, is flush with the ceiling, adding considerable height to the bed. The feeling of enclosure continues at the windows where folding shutters can totally mask the outside. Consistent with all the other rooms, the windows have period molding. Consistency—of vision, sentiment, and personal style—is, in fact, the theme running through this house.

191

living in a
french country style

The Atlanta house
could be just as at home in
France (right). Its tall
front doors have a topiary
basket of ivy with
pink impatiens. The doorframe
and facade are
purposely antiquated to be in
character with
European manor houses.

The living room's
tied slipcovers and puddled
curtains (opposite) give
it a summer air. It is fragrant.
too, considering the
large basket of eucalyptus.

Unlike people, rooms aren't born with a heritage: They acquire it through decoration. Yet the style a room takes on originates somewhere, perhaps from a fantasy or an idealized place or the breeding of the house. In Atlanta, Georgia, there is a house that looks French born and bred, from its stucco exterior and paved courtyard to its hip roof. Those evocative elements inspired the decoration which is as characteristic of France as a field of lavender.

The cultivation of French style came naturally to the owner, whose business took her there on a regular basis. For Atlanta designer Nancy Braithwaite, the house and its new owner were of the same mind. Even before they began to decorate, the house projected a nineteenth-century French country style.

Ms. Braithwaite used restraint in decorating, her concept being that there should be no distraction from rooms with what professionals consider good bones. Ac-

cessories, therefore, are few enough to count at first glance; the furniture big enough to have an impact. That's how to avoid clutter. "It takes a long time to learn this," says the designer, citing the tendency to start out with too many small objects. The graduation from that stage of decorating to her level of confidence is what separates the novice from the professional.

What contributes to the authentic French accent of its rooms are the details, imported from no farther than Georgia. Courtyard cobblestones came from old city streets; ceiling beams from the roundhouse at the Atlanta railroad terminal; brick for the floors from sidewalks in Decatur; the dining-room mantle from a local house; leaded-glass windows from a downtown mansion. To preserve the inherent quality of old French houses, the designer used what she calls "noncolors," painting and glazing walls in gray with deeper woodwork. By using the same color scheme from room to room, with slight variation in shades, she pays respect to the consistency of style and spirit. Consistency also reigns when it comes to materials, which are linen and cotton throughout. Where there are curtains, they are mostly organdy made in simple pleated panels and hung to emphasize the height of the windows. Therefore, the rods are often above the window frame and close to the ceiling. This emphasis on verticality is to Braithwaite the critical ingredient of decorating because it establishes a new line of vision and elevates the

192

whole room. The same concept was applied to a canopy bed, its tall frame treated as if it were curtain rods, with organdy fabric hung to the floor.

The theory of buying furniture to last a lifetime is illustrated here. Banquettes from an earlier home, for example, were given thick cushions and easy-fitting slip-covers with ties. And the dining chairs, whose original seats were wrapped down, received stylish new covers.

What has been achieved in the thoughtful decorating of this house can best be described in a single word of no other than French origin—finesse.

Rose bushes, 130 strong, grow close to the house in European fashion (top). French doors open out to the garden allowing intimate views.

The family room also has French doors (above) and is accessible from the garden where herbs and flowers can be picked for winter drying.

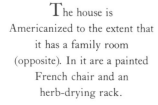

The house is Americanized to the extent that it has a family room (opposite). In it are a painted French chair and an herb-drying rack.

The family room's fireplace (above left) recalls French country houses, with its masonry wall and dark wood mantel. The rustic brick floor contributes further to the room's ambience.

195

As with so many of the rooms, the kitchen has access to a garden (right). Plant care takes place on a French blue tile counter near the kitchen sink (far right).

The dining room
(right) was painted in what
the designer calls
"noncolors." The walls were
glazed in a gray tone,
a darker version of which colors
the woodwork and
fireplace mantel, as well as its
mirror. Old garden urns
are appreciated in their weathered
state, rust and all.

The dining room's
French doors were made to
appear taller with the
addition of glass panels
above them (right).
Draperies hung flush with the
molding accentuate
the height. Made of organdy
and banded with
cotton, they hang from thin
iron rods.

The kitchen
(opposite below) has leaded
glass windows from a
mansion in the area. For the
cooktop to be angled
in the corner required a
hood designed to
correspond. Wood cabinets were
painted and glazed
when the counter tiles were
chosen.

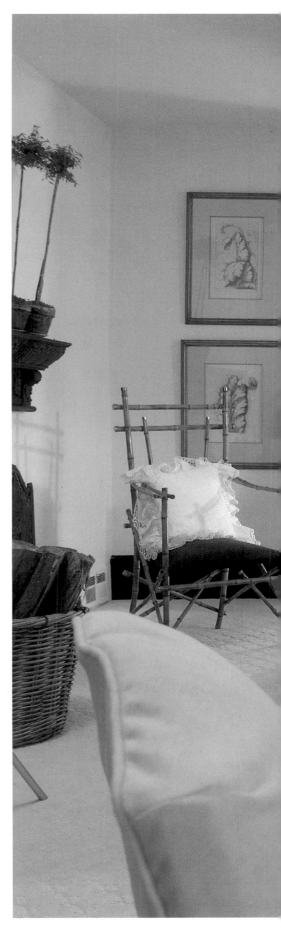

The living room's
coffee table (above) was made
from 18th-century
French paving stones. It sits
between matching
sofas slipcovered in the French
manner, slightly loose
fitted and tied.

The bedroom (right)
has its height accentuated with
an iron four-poster.
Positioned on the diagonal to
focus on the fireplace,
the bed has a canopy of checked
organdy that ties like
slipcovers. The bed and window
curtains are of similar
fabric. A French laundry
hamper borders the
bed with dried baby's breath.

character in a new house

A small house (left) is treated as if it were grand with a framed entrance, lattice trim, and steep roof. The V-shaped bay window brings light down into the entryway.

When decorator and architect take on a small space with equal enthusiasm and respect for each other's ability, harmony results. One such successful collaboration is evident in a 1,500-square-foot house designed by Connecticut architects Shope Reno Wharton Associates and decorated by Mariette Himes Gomez of New York. Rather than being restricted by the small size, the team turned resourceful, using imaginative and practical means to open up rooms. For example, height was implied with the vertical design of the house, a style reminiscent of turn-of-the-century cottages. Architect Bernard Wharton refers to the pitched roofline as being in the cottage tradition and giving the house a sense of presence. "The house feels grander through the use of materials," he says, noting the wood lattice trim and cedar roof shingles with weathered copper inserts. Views also give the house its big image, from both outside in and vice versa. An imaginative variety of windows open the house from many angles and give it architectural distinction as well. The only

The entry has a shaft
of light from above: a large
mirror helps expand
the space (right), as does the
pale wood floor.
Furniture is centered in the
living room (below)
to give a sense of spaciousness.

Generous seating
favors the fireplace (above)
which is uplit by a
pair of sconces that blend with
the wall. An area rug
anchors the furniture and
introduces pattern
that, like the pillows, brings a
feeling of antiquity to
a new house.

201

The interaction of kitchen with dining room is both informal and gracious due to the traditional fireplace and round table with 18th-century-style chairs (below). The view extends across the cooktop to French doors and the garden, a bonus for the chef.

reason for covering certain windows would be for privacy, which is the reason Ms. Gomez chose opaque shades and simple curtains where necessary. Her sensitivity to the architecture is evident in all aspects of the interior design, from the choice of color to the placement of furniture.

This cohesion of architecture and interior design, an age-old issue, comes up in *The Decoration of Houses*, a book whose author, Edith Wharton, happens to be distantly related to the architect. In 1902, she and co-author Ogden

Codman, Jr. wrote: "Those who employ different people to build and decorate their houses should at least try to select an architect and decorator trained in the same school of composition, so that they may come to some understanding with regard to the general harmony of their work."

There is a mutual attitude in this small house, as noted by Ms. Gomez, who, along with the architects, intended to create an illusion of space. She reinforced the verticality of the architecture with deft use of color, pattern, and scale. In

Angled windows over the sink (top) give a bigger dimension to the work area and infuse it with light. The deep window ledge serves as a miniature greenhouse. Pale pine cabinets (above) are practical and nonobtrusive; glass fronts break up the mass of wood.

One compact bedroom (right) draws light from a small soffit window, which matches those on all corners of the house. Curtains and valance are of muted stripes to quietly blend with the room's antique textiles and American antiques.

Windows in the main bedroom (below) have horizontally pleated opaque shades for privacy and fabric to match the bed skirt. The beaded ceiling curves upward to 11 feet and suggests a canopy over the bed. It also provides space for an imposing highboy.

The spare room or study, a compact 10 by 10 feet, gains substance through its decorating (left). A chaise that could double as a guest bed and a roomy upholstered chair take full advantage of the window and its view. Pale tones, including the sisal rug, and limited accessories keep the room from feeling confined.

The main bathroom (below) owes its spacious quality to pale tile walls and a built-in vanity. A big expanse of mirror convinces the eye of doubled space.

the case of color, white with cream-toned trim helps rooms appear "almost double in size," according to the designer, who specified China White and Linen White (Benjamin Moore paints). Regarding scale, the concept of bigger-is-better is applied. By that she means generous proportions as in the living room sofa, a 36-inch-high model instead of the usual 32 inches. A generously scaled highboy in the main bedroom is another case in point. It also illustrates the harmony between architecture and interior design, the curved piece being chosen for its reference to the curved ceiling. The architect's response? He sees a new perspective on the bedroom, its beaded ceiling forming a sort of canopy over the traditional four-poster. Compliments are due to the interior designer for her clever choice of furnishings that pay respect to the architecture.

a home
in a gristmill

At its most creative level, decorating is theater. Part improvisation, part thoughtful preparation, but theater. The stage, in this case, is a former gristmill on Virginia's Cacotin Creek. The players, Ed Bouchard and Bud Yeck, poured their energies into the abandoned eighteenth-century building even after discovering that the mill's history included floods. Being professionals in the design business, the two were versed in crisis intervention. What they did to control the floods was to build an earth island with 50 truckloads of landfill, thereby gaining a gently sloping lawn and room for a kitchen terrace. From then on, they unleashed their creativity.

The mill became an arena where decorating was more improvisational than traditional. "We didn't feel we had to decorate in an American primitive style," says Mr. Bouchard, "just because we were in an American primitive building." The biggest testament to their free style is in the living room, a 20-by-50-foot area that would challenge the most confident of decorators. The very dark beamed ceiling had a very dark wood floor dragging it down and absorbing much of the light. Rather than subdue the ceiling, they deemphasized the floor by staining the pine a pale blond. That the ceiling was original, "wonderfully mellow" chestnut beams and the floor was new, ordinary pine contributed to their decision. Besides, the dark beams had a provincial French feeling the owners wanted to preserve and use as a counterpoint for light furnishings. To lighten the floor, the owners used a stain and paint referred to as platinum which required several applications in order to diminish the pine's natural yellow cast. The floor demanded additional coats because of its highly absorbent nature. Its final layer was satin-finish gym seal for protection with minimum gloss. Because of the way the floor was lit, there appears to be greater distance between it and the ceiling. The ceiling's light comes from high-intensity track spots, with eight of them on one beam over the dining table—the same as the number of guests accommodated.

The stone gate, gristmill, and terrace (above) honor the original structure. Antique pineapple finials are symbols of welcome. The terrace is covered by a trellis custom-made of 2-by-2 cedar, which grays as it weathers. A plastic awning, inspired by one at the local zoo, drops down in winter. One end of the living room has a sisal rug as pale as the floor (opposite). The floating steps are dark like the original chestnut beams, with all the fabrics white cotton to make light prevail.

206

In the process of introducing more light to the room, the designers changed windows and recycled columns bought from a display company. The columns were plastered, painted white, and installed next to walls that a decorative painter transformed into what appears to be white stone. Because nothing was square in the room, the painter had to approach the walls from an abstract perspective. The room's size posed another problem, that of furniture placement to make the space seem less cavernous. Accomplishing that triggered more theatrics. Dual situations were created, an idea based on mirror image. So where there is a table on one side of the room, an opposing table appears. Similarly, there are columns on either side. The duplication is hardly monotonous, a feat considering the sameness of color. What makes the room lyrical is its diversity of textures and shapes. A round table swathed in a fringed white cloth sits near a rough stone fireplace original to the building. Wicker sits next to wood and terra-cotta pots, with an eclectic group of accessories as focal points. Because of all the white and the finely edited furnishings, every detail is highly visible. Here a table made of deer antlers, there an alabaster urn.

The octagonal table (right) is always covered in a floor-length cloth matching the seat cushions. A Giacometti-style chandelier centers on the table. The antler table, used as a console, is said to be Scottish, c. 1840. Twin pillars (above) have the same exterior quality as the wall, which is painted to mimic stone.

The upstairs is another living quarter, based on the theme of duplication. For example, it too has beams as well as a sitting room and fireplace. And it is predominantly white. Where it differs is in its coziness, a quality the owners wanted for the most lived-in area. The spaces, therefore, are smaller, with more concentration of upholstered furniture to reinforce the warmth. When the weather turns warm, upholstery that would normally be paisley is slipcovered in white cotton. The guest room, a mere 7 by 11 feet, is theater also, a botanical garden of sorts with ivy painted around its window. A total departure from the rest of the house, the room is rich with pattern, which the designers claim enhances the scale. They say the pattern actually furnishes the room.

Dual purpose was also a consideration in decorating the guest room. The desk is also the bed's end table; the ottoman a chair as well. The armoire is both a guest closet and linen storage. The actual closet holds a washer and dryer, a nerve center for the whole house.

More cerebral endeavors take place in the library where busts of author Mary Shelley and her husband, poet Percy Bysshe Shelley, preside. Antlers appear upstairs, too, on a plaster deerhead with a garland. The antlers are real; the deerhead started out brown until Bud Yeck decided to white it out. This is yet another example of creative license that made home of a gristmill and theater of decorating.

Upstairs is a library
(opposite) whose paisley-
upholstered seats
are changed to white cotton
slipcovers in summer.

Another section of
the library (above left) has an
oriental screen as its
artwork.

The guest
room (left and above) has
sponge-painted walls
with real-looking ivy climbing
around the windows.
Four Minton plates hang above
the bed carved to look
like bamboo and said to come
from a Stanford
White house. What links the
diverse fabric patterns
is the essentially blue color
scheme.

211

rescuing a historic home

An intriguing
facade, combined of brick and
clapboard (right),
includes a new bay window.

The dining room
(opposite) has as its focal
point a group of
Nymphenburg plates from the
German porcelain
factory. Black dominates the
wall, which displays jet-colored
urns, an abstract
painting, and an old tapestry.
Black is also
prominent on the crystal and
iron chandelier.
French doors to the garden
often stay open.

Houses, too, are prone to mid-life crises. And fifty is a susceptible age. The usual symptoms include wrinkles on the walls, wear marks on the carpet, shadows on the ceiling. The cure can be cosmetic or more ambitious structural changes. With the half-century-old house in one of Atlanta's prestigious neighborhoods, the changes ran the whole gamut—two years' worth of revamping and rejuvenating. All because it was so charming to begin with, "you wanted to hum," says Dan Carithers, the owner, whose profession is design and whose vision instilled new vigor into the house.

"Not a fine house, but charming" is how Carithers describes the place before and after its transformation. His intention was to preserve the old charm so that all the changes would be seamless, and it would be as livable as it formerly appeared. Insofar as major changes, the house is almost a recycling of itself. Windows removed from one area were used in another. The same for beams and doors. The owners' tendency to waste not became an active part of the decorating process, which included using fabric, wallpaper, and furnishings stored away for years.

One favored piece of furniture, a 45-inch-high antique daybed, actually was responsible for the building of a bay window. The newly created alcove bathes the sofa in light, and because of the unusual height of the upholstered frame, it provides enclosure and privacy from the street. Its original horsehair mattress and down cushions render the piece enormously comfortable for sitting or curling up with a book, a well-earned pastime for Mr. Carithers.

The energy expended in decorating was intense, a planned and concentrated effort that involved the entire ten-room house, including a new kitchen, library, and bedroom for the Carithers' son. While some homeowners would opt for a less ambitious makeover, that is, a project this year, one the next, the Carithers went full speed ahead. Momentum grew from their combined creativity. He, for example, had saved some raw silk whose buff color turned out to be ideal for the living room windows. That he had a limited supply of the 36-inch fabric inspired resourcefulness. Off to the workroom he went holding a handkerchief by one corner: "This is the way the curtain should

213

hang, and this is all the fabric I have." The relaxed style he achieved is a kind of swag with insouciance.

Relaxation is an important footnote to this house, and somewhat of a paradox considering the degree of labor put forth. Yet, the life expressed in the Carithers' living room and, indeed, in all the house is imaginative, aesthetic, and obviously thoughtful. The kitchen, as an example, has a Welsh lambing chair for visitors, its large bottom drawer a catchall for sundry papers having to do with appliances and receipts. Hardly a day goes by that someone doesn't sit in the chair. Its attraction, other than being strategic to the cooking, is that it echoes. For the cook's convenience, an iron rack hangs over the work island. Every pot on it is used on a regular basis.

The library invites staying and perusing. Here, according to Mr. Carithers, "nothing matches." He cites a chest from Italy, horn chairs and table from England, and a dimensional map from Paris. "Like buying books" is how he describes the development of this room enriched with the stuff of travel and curiosity. The evidence of avid collectors is not confined to the library. A dozen antique plates hang in the dining room; another group of plates— all brown and white—appears on the kitchen wall. Fabric is another aspect of their collecting. One, an ivy pattern that had been stashed away, was recruited for assorted chairs, two of which were garage-sale bargains. The chairs spent five years at an upholsterer waiting for the right moment. They, like the house, got a second chance.

The entrance hall (right) has antlers as a rack for collected straw hats. Its railing was painted with white epoxy, the hardest finish available. Rustic beams contrast with the smooth floor and shiny banister.

The far end of the kitchen (far right) houses a collection of Staffordshire, Wedgewood, and Spode with brown and white as the common denominator. Ivy is another theme illustrated by the chair fabrics and topiaries. Green repeats in the metal shades and tassels of the candlestick lamps.

The library (right) is eclectic in its assortment of furnishings found on European trips. Nothing matches except for a pair of bookshelves flanking the fireplace and a set of white andirons.

The kitchen work area (opposite) contains beams that had formerly been in a North Carolina church. When purchased, they measured 41 feet long and were cut to fit as the room was remodeled. The hard pine floor got its tone from one-half rosewood, one-half black coffee stain. Utilitarian antiques— a Welsh lambing chair, pine plate rack, and farm table—make the room feel lived in.

The dimensions of the living room were transformed (left) with the addition of a bay window and faux-marble paint on the fireplace wall. Mr. Carithers considered the original fireplace too big; therefore he aimed to heighten the room's appearance by treating the whole wall as one piece of furniture. Its color was derived from the creamware collection on the mantel. Panels made from antique Chinese wallpaper color the room further.

Boiserie from the 18th century acts as a mirror frame (above), over which is a ribbon, not for support but for decoration. Underneath, a French chest serves as a side table for drinks and a display case for matching urns and candle lamps.

The master bedroom (left) has toile from France, a bench from South Carolina, a spread found in England, and a mirror bought at a local estate sale. Artwork above the headboard is framed by bamboo-style wood in an abbreviated canopy.

Large black-and-white tiles magnify the size of a small powder room (above). The miniature Gothic chair was left in its original finish—as found on an antiques excursion.

DIRECTORY OF
DESIGNERS AND ARCHITECTS

Leslie Allen
Westport, Connecticut

Beinfield Wagner & Associates
Norwalk, Connecticut

Freya Block
New York, New York

Ed Bouchard
Leesburg, Virginia

Nancy Braithwaite
Atlanta, Georgia

Mario Buatta
New York, New York

Dan Carithers
Atlanta, Georgia

Sandy Ceppos
New Canaan, Connecticut

George Constant
New York, New York

Gary Crain
New York, New York

Mary Douglas Drysdale
Washington, D.C.

Ann Dupuy
New Orleans, Louisiana

Gep Durenberger
San Juan Capistrano, California

Beverly Ellsley
Westport, Connecticut

Georgina Fairholme
New York, New York

Simone Feldman
New York, New York

Nelson Ferlita
New York, New York

Toby Flax
Alexander Valley, California

Tom Fleming
New York, New York

Mariette Himes Gomez
New York, New York

Carolyn Guttilla
Locust Valley, New York

Victoria Hagan
New York, New York

Mark Hampton
New York, New York

Nan Heminway
Litchfield, Connecticut

William Hodgins
Boston, Massachusetts

Ann Holden
New Orleans, Louisiana

Keith Irvine
New York, New York

Hugh Newell Jacobsen
Washington, D.C.

Lynn Jacobson
New York, New York

Carlos Jimenez
Houston, Texas

Richard Langham
New York, New York

Robert K. Lewis
New York, New York

Stephen Mallory
New York, New York

Ron Mann
San Francisco, California

Ned Marshall
New York, New York

Anne Mullen Interiors
Greenwich, Connecticut

Richard Lowell Neas
New York, New York

Lyn Peterson
New Rochelle, New York

Nancy Goslee Power
Santa Monica, California

Tom Rose
Hadlyme, Connecticut

John Saladino
New York, New York

Harry Schule
New York, New York

Stephen Shubel
San Francisco, California

Michael Taylor
San Francisco, California

Shope Reno Wharton Associates
Greenwich, Connecticut

Peter Wheeler
Boston, Massachusetts

Bud Yeck
Leesburg, Virginia

Zajac and Callahan
New York, New York

PHOTOGRAPHY CREDITS